# *Private Passage*

*Private Passage* is a courageous and artful exploration of a woman's personal process of deciding to be a mother and the family and systems that she must navigate to choose what's right for her. As a director of this production, the creative opportunities it afforded actors and designers were unparalleled. The conversations we had with our audiences were thrillingly complicated and opened up a challenging but necessary space for people to share their experiences with this fraught and painful issue.

Jessi D. Hill

director of the Stage Left (Chicago)
production of *Private Passage*

# *Private Passage*

**A play by**
**Louise Bylicki**
**&**
**James Serpento**

**KINGMAN ROW ENTERTAINMENT**
**JOHNSTON, IOWA**

James Serpento
KINGMAN ROW ENTERTAINMENT, LLC
5919 Greendale Place; #101    Johnston, IA; 50131
515-321-1507    navarre_2@yahoo.com

*Published and printed in the United States of America*

ISBN-13: 978-0-9960746-8-1
Library of Congress Control Number: 2020921889

Cover image and cover design by Laura Jordan. Laura
Jordan's cover image is protected by all applicable copyrights.
It is available for use by producing groups in their own
marketing materials. Please contact Kingman Row
Entertainment, LLC for terms.

Production Coordinator: Heidi Bibler

The play is dedicated, in loving memory, to
Mr. Russ Tutterow of Chicago, Illinois

*Private Passage* was commissioned by Lynne DuFresne, Artistic Director of Odyssey Theatre, and developed at Chicago Dramatists (Russ Tutterow, Artistic Director). The play was first produced by Odyssey Theatre, in cooperation with the Equity Library Showcase Code, at Facets Multimedia in Chicago, Illinois. The first performance was September 24, 1991. The play was produced by Ms. DuFresne and the late Nicklas Gray (Executive Director of Odyssey Theatre).

The production was directed by Shannon Cochran. Scenic design was by Joe Gluekert and Judith Austin, with lights by Debbie Sander, sound and original music by David Zerlin, and costumes by Nanette Acosta. The stage manager was Sam Patterson. The cast was as follows:

| | |
|---|---|
| Drew | LYNNE DUFRESNE |
| 1st Woman | ROBIN KERSEY |
| 2nd Woman | DEANNA DUNAGAN |
| 3rd Woman | JESSICA FRANKEL |
| 1st Man | PETER MORANGE |
| 2nd Man | BRIAN HORTON |
| 3rd Man | MARK ST. AMANT |

Both Ms. Kersey and Ms. Dunagan were nominated for Joseph Jefferson Awards for their performances.

Following a substantial rewrite, the play was revived by Stage Left Theatre Company, in a production directed by Jessi D. Hill, which opened on January 11, 2000. Scenic design was by Ms. Hill and Aaron Mitchell, with lights by Leigh Barrett, sound by Chris J. Johnson, and costumes by Cathy Valladares and Barbara Carnahan White. The assistant director was David M. Schmitz and the production stage manager was Leigh Barrett. The cast was as follows:

| | |
|---|---|
| Drew | STACY STOLTZ |
| 1st Woman | LYDIA BERGER |
| 2nd Woman | SUSAN FERRARA |
| 3rd Woman | MICHELLE K. GOODMAN |
| 1st Man | LARRY DAHLKE |
| 2nd Man | REID J. ROBINSON |
| 3rd Man | DEREK RICHARD SMART |

In 2018, the play was selected for the Scriptease program at Iowa Stage Theatre Company of Des Moines, Iowa (Matthew McIver, Artistic Director) and the current, updated version of the script contained herein was produced in July, 2019, by Kingman Row Entertainment, in association with Iowa Stage Theatre Company's Launch Program, at the Kum n Go Theatre (Daniel Haymes, liaison).

The production was produced by Kathy Hellstern and directed by James Serpento, with lighting design by Dakota Sommer and sound design by Joshua Jepson. The stage manager was Amanda Keesling and the assistant director was Kimi Reed. The cast was as follows:

| | |
|---|---|
| Drew | HEIDI BIBLER |
| 1st Woman | MAGGIE JANE TATONE |
| 2nd Woman | JENNIFER K.D. HUGHES |
| 3rd Woman | DESHANA LANGFORD |
| 1st Man | ERIC OLSON |
| 2nd Man | JOHN AUDLEHELM |
| 3rd Man | MICHAEL TALLMAN |

## *CHARACTERS*

**DREW.**  A young woman. Alternates between the ages of 14 and 24 years old. This role is not combined with any other in the play.

### THE ENSEMBLE OF THREE WOMEN AND THREE MEN:

#### 1ST WOMAN
PHOEBE
KELLY (A STUDENT)

#### 2ND WOMAN
THE MOTHER
WOMAN VISITING THE BUREAU
1ST WOMAN IN A BUREAU OFFICE

#### 3RD WOMAN
JESSICA
FRANNIE
COUNSELOR (GRACE)
2ND WOMAN IN A BUREAU OFFICE
CLOWN 3
A CHILD

#### 1ST MAN
JIMMY (A STUDENT)
THE FATHER
CLOWN 2
THE JUDGE

#### 2ND MAN
A STUDENT
PHOEBE'S BOYFRIEND
THE MAN IN ROOM TWO
PETER FRANKLIN (BLAH-BLAH)
CLOWN 1
A DOCTOR

#### 3RD MAN
BOBBY
A PREACHER
A POLITICIAN

Some other roles in the text are identified only by the number of the ENSEMBLE MEMBER.

The role of THE JUDGE may be played by a woman, if so desired by a particular company.

Any other roles having no particular designation can be assigned according to the taste of the individual director and acting company.

### SETTING

The setting should be as simple and transformable as possible. Changes in location should be accomplished with lighting, and through the actions and transformations of the actors.

# Act One

# PRIVATE PASSAGE

## A play by
## Louise Bylicki and James Serpento

### ACT ONE

*(Music. Light rises on the ENSEMBLE MEMBERS. DREW speaks, as the other ENSEMBLE MEMBERS begin to move.)*

**DREW:** When I was a little girl, I saw that my mother was a big girl with a little girl who was me.

When I was a little girl, I heard that I would grow up, get married and have children, just the way that the big girl who held my hand had done.

When I grew up, that thought became a coffee-cloud because I was busy growing up. . .

**2ND WOMAN:** The most dangerous place in America

**1ST MAN:** that we know of, at any rate

**2ND WOMAN:** is inside a mother's womb

**1ST WOMAN:** inside me

**DREW:** inside me

**ALL WOMEN:** inside us

1

**ENSEMBLE:** inside a woman

**1ST WOMAN:** stop

**2ND MAN:** stop?

**1ST WOMAN:** end it

**2ND WOMAN:** no, say it

**DREW:** stop end

**2ND WOMAN:** no, say it

**3RD MAN:** say it

**3RD WOMAN:** say the word

**1ST WOMAN:** Say what? Say what? Are you *accusing* me?

**DREW:** Then one day in a grown-up wintertime, I was sitting alone at a café. I looked outside, a car drove by, churned up the driven snow, until it became the color of light brown sugar. *(Pause.)* Cookie dough snow. . .

**3RD WOMAN:** Now, you know what is true. I know

**DREW:** what is true is
    I saw, I saw with such beautiful clarity
    Myself as a big girl with a little girl at my side
    Tiny bundled creature, round wet eyes
    A fawn's eyes
    My eyes

**3RD MAN:** No, say it

*(1ST WOMAN — as PHOEBE — utters a high-pitched sound: a wailing that might also be the beginning of a song. Then silence.)*

**3RD WOMAN:** Once upon a time

**DREW:** I see myself telling her the story of
    Cookie Dough Snow:

**2ᴺᴰ WOMAN:** in a time come upon us like rain

**3ᴿᴰ WOMAN:** across a fruitful land, made great again, yes

**DREW:** Wonderful web of a tale spun from the treads of dirty tires

**3ᴿᴰ WOMAN:** for something is inside me

**2ᴺᴰ WOMAN:** growing inside me

**1ˢᵀ WOMAN:** and dare we ask

**3ᴿᴰ WOMAN:** "Do I want. . .?"

**DREW:** I want to be a mother, I knew I would be a mother

**2ᴺᴰ WOMAN:** and who pays?

**DREW:** Someday

**2ᴺᴰ WOMAN:** at a time like this. . . ?

**3ᴿᴰ WOMAN:** this is my question

**2ᴺᴰ WOMAN:** this creature, yes

**3ᴿᴰ WOMAN:** who pays with their *life?*

**1ˢᵀ MAN:** this life, yes, but

**DREW:** Is that today?

**PHOEBE** *(sings)*: I COULD BE THE PRESIDENT

**2ᴺᴰ WOMAN:** this patch of blood and tissue

**3ᴿᴰ WOMAN:** this soul bright of blee

**DREW:** Why am I thinking what I am thinking?

**PHOEBE** *(sings)*: I COULD BE A FOOL

**2ᴺᴰ MAN:** Case Number 4356-12D75

**3<sup>RD</sup> WOMAN** *(overlaps)***:** got no fuckin' money, how the fuck I'm s'pose'ta raise a *kid?*

**DREW:** How must it feel, to have your arm ripped away? What must it feel like to dissolve? Oh God. . .

**3<sup>RD</sup> MAN:** Case Number 13HB5-2W778

**2<sup>ND</sup> WOMAN** *(overlaps)***:** I'm twelve years old!

**DREW:** And how do we *know?*

**3<sup>RD</sup> WOMAN:** We're pregnant!

**3<sup>RD</sup> MAN:** and I can't stop smiling

**1<sup>ST</sup> MAN:** Case Number 80175-64591BDW914

**2<sup>ND</sup> WOMAN** *(overlaps)***:** he is drunk, he kicks the living *daylights* out of me every night, I don't want his *filth* inside of me, tell me he can sue for *custody*, motherfucker, *FUCK YOU!*

**PHOEBE** *(sings)***:** I COULD MAKE A CRAZY WORLD
A LITTLE BETTER, WHO KNOWS?

**DREW:** How do I know they don't scream?

**PHOEBE** *(sings)***:** FOR SOMEONE LIKE ME
WHO KNOWS?

**2<sup>ND</sup> WOMAN:** We have four beautiful children. . .

**PHOEBE** *(sings)***:** WERE IT NOT

**2<sup>ND</sup> WOMAN** *(overlapping)***:** . . .already

**3<sup>RD</sup> MAN:** Case Number 9153-501-ABK-74442

**PHOEBE** *(sings, overlapping)***:** FOR SOMEONE LIKE ME

**2<sup>ND</sup> MAN:** Case Number 1212-5309-617-ZYX-34892

**3<sup>RD</sup> WOMAN** *(overlapping)***:** He *raped* me

**2ND WOMAN:** And he's going to be its daddy?

**1ST MAN:** In this state

**2ND WOMAN:** What kind of *monster*

**DREW:** Who's to say?

**PHOEBE** *(sings)*: I WILL PLAY MY INSTRUMENT

**1ST MAN:** Case Number 3TX-2029LKW-3KKYAHO-XX-BB-ZED

**2ND WOMAN** *(overlapping)*: He is my father

**2ND MAN:** Case Number 16390-4897-POB-182-KLAB74651

**2ND WOMAN** *(overlapping)*: I can't *have* children!
 Ungrateful, spiteful, barren

**3RD WOMAN:** send another'n to school, that *shit*hole metal detectin' motherfucker, I just bought my oldes' a goddamn bulletproof *ves'*, you jes' *go* on now, get yourself *good* and fucked

**PHOEBE** *(sings)*: AS I'VE ALWAYS WANTED TO

**2ND MAN:** Case Number 55507261-LAU-84-44-444-44440 - XX-YY-ABC

**1ST MAN** *(overlapping)*: You don't understand

**3RD WOMAN:** I'm not meant to be a mother

**2ND WOMAN:** I'll hurt it

**3RD WOMAN:** I can't love it

**2ND WOMAN:** I can't protect it

**3RD MAN:** we have no home

*(The 1ST MAN and 2ND WOMAN turn to each other suddenly.)*

**1ST MAN** and **2ND WOMAN**: *I can't live with you anymore!*

**3RD WOMAN** *(front)*: gon' *pay* my fuckin' bills, mister?

**PHOEBE** *(sings)*: I WILL DO A MILLION THINGS

**3RD WOMAN**: You fill this prescription, pal, it's your *job*

**DREW**: Dear God, is there an answer to this?

**1ST MAN**: Case Number 132-H, deceased.

**2ND MAN** *(overlaps)*: Case Number 571-B9, deceased, the uterine wall has been punctured

**3RD WOMAN**: she has bled to death

**2ND MAN**: Jesus, I think

**3RD MAN**: me, too

**1ST MAN**: me, too

**2ND MAN**: I'm going to be sick. . .

*(Beat.)*

**1ST MAN**: Well, *some*body has to pull it out of there

**3RD WOMAN**: She is thirty-four years old

**3RD MAN**: Christ, she's a kid, look at this

**2ND MAN**: What is she, thirteen?

**3RD WOMAN**: *Yes*, it hurts. Teenagers' hips aren't meant for childbearin', and that'll teach you, won't it. Now, bite down on this

**3RD MAN**: oh, my God, she's burned everything

**3RD WOMAN**: can't be more than seventeen years old

*(PHOEBE kneels, her back to the audience. She raises a long, thin, sharp object slowly into the air.)*

6

**2ND MAN:** what *happened* here?

**1ST MAN:** Case Number 376-18

**2ND MAN:** I regret to inform you

**DREW** *(in her sleep)***:** Who are these people, Mama?

*(BOBBY turns to look at DREW, then stares front again, looking at a television. PHOEBE sinks into a heap on the floor.)*

**FATHER:** Who are you?

**MOTHER:** that's my daughter

**DREW**: Phoebe?

**2ND MAN:** your daughter is

**MOTHER:** my daughter is dead, is that what you're saying to me?

**DREW**: Mama

**MOTHER:** which of you knew about this?

**2ND MAN:** I regret to inform you

**FATHER:** inform us of what?

**MOTHER:** my daughter is, what are you *saying*?

**3RD WOMAN:** regret to inform you

**MOTHER:** where is my, oh my god, my

**2ND MAN:** regret

**MOTHER:** my *child*?

**3RD WOMAN:** regret

**2ND MAN:** regret

**3<sup>RD</sup> WOMAN:** regret

**MOTHER:** *WHO HAS KILLED MY BABY?!*

**DREW** *(waking suddenly):* Mama. . . ?

*(Silence. The ENSEMBLE retreats into the shadows, leaving DREW and BOBBY alone. Television sounds continue, under.)*

**BOBBY:** You okay?

*(Silence.)*

**DREW:** Yes.

**BOBBY:** You were talking again.

**DREW:** I'm sorry.

**BOBBY:** Ssh. *(Pause.)* Is the TV bothering you?

**DREW:** No.

**BOBBY:** It's just, I love this show. New season just started. I can't go to sleep yet. Want some popcorn? There's no salt on it.

**DREW:** No. I'm. . .I'm going to try to sleep again, okay? *(Pause.)* Do you want to make love?

**BOBBY:** I always want to make love with you.

**DREW** *(pause):* It's Netflix, right?

**BOBBY** *(pause):* Uh-huh.

**DREW** *(pause):* We can wait till it's over.

**BOBBY:** You sure?

**DREW:** Wake me up when it's over, okay?

**BOBBY:** Okay.

**DREW:** Bobby?

**BOBBY:** Hm?

**DREW:** We're gonna be old someday.

**BOBBY:** Uh-huh.

**DREW:** Do you want someone else? I mean, before you get old?

**BOBBY:** Nope.

**DREW:** Oh. *(Pause.)* I'm going to get ugly, I bet, when I get old.

**BOBBY:** Uh-huh. I'll get fat and we'll be even. *(Pause.)*

**DREW:** Bobby?

**BOBBY:** Uh-huh?

**DREW** *(sleepy)***:** Do you wanna get married?

**BOBBY:** Right now?

**DREW:** Someday.

**BOBBY:** Do I have to get dressed up?

**DREW:** Yes. In a tux and everything. Do you want to?

**BOBBY:** Do *you* want to?

**DREW:** I was asking you first.

**BOBBY:** I want to be with you. Okay? That's all I care about. *(Pause.)* That and this show.

**DREW** *(laughs sleepily)***:** Jerk.

**BOBBY:** What? Honesty is important in any relationship.

*(BOBBY holds out his hand, little finger extended. DREW entwines her little finger in his and she closes her eyes. Pause. PHOEBE approaches.)*

**PHOEBE:** Don't be scared.

9

**DREW** *(wakes; light laughter)***:** I'm not scared of you, why would I be?

*(No response from PHOEBE.)*

**DREW:** Oh. Because you're dead?

**PHOEBE:** Yeah. Want me to be a ghost or an angel?

**DREW:** A ghost. No, an angel. No, wait, a ghost, no—

**PHOEBE** *(laughs)***:** An angel, then, mush-head. I'm an angel. Blessed be me!

*(DREW laughs, as PHOEBE moves happily around the room.)*

**PHOEBE:** One sweet and low-down angel, that's me! Blessed be!

**DREW:** Blessed be!

*(PHOEBE lights near the bed. She and DREW giggle, then fall silent.)*

**DREW:** I like angels.

**PHOEBE** *(nods)***:** There are lots of us. Billions and zillions.

**DREW:** Nice ones?

**PHOEBE** *(nods)***:** And funny ones. *(Pause.)* My little baby sister.

**DREW:** Not a baby. Twenty-four.

**PHOEBE:** I would be. . .

**DREW:** . . .twenty-six.

**PHOEBE:** Can you think of it? I wonder what my face would look like.

*(DREW suddenly burbles into tears. BOBBY notices this, but does not acknowledge PHOEBE.)*

**DREW:** I miss you, oh. . .

**PHOEBE:** Ssh, now. . .blessed be. . .

**DREW** *(calming a little)*: . . .blessed be. . .

**PHOEBE** *(placing a hand on DREW's belly)*: . . .blessed be you, baby. . .

*(Silence.)*

**DREW:** What. . . ?

**PHOEBE:** Just remember. . .

**DREW:** . . . what are you saying. . . ?

**PHOEBE** *(smiles gently)*: I can come to you here. In your mind. And I'll help you remember.

**DREW:** I don't want to. . .

**PHOEBE:** . . .you have to. You have to remember where you've been—

**MOTHER** *(off)*: Drew!

**PHOEBE:** —to know where you're going. . .

**MOTHER** *(entering)*: Drew?

**DREW** *(suddenly younger)*: Here, Mama!

**MOTHER:** Done yet?

**DREW:** No, I just got home from school, is Phoebe home?

**MOTHER:** She has band practice, now, these signs. . .

**DREW** *(happily)*: I know, I know, I know.

**MOTHER:** You know. I *hear* that you know, I don't *see* that you know. You're the artist around here, so get to work.

*(DREW flops down on the floor and begins writing, as though making a large poster.)*

**MOTHER:** Did you have a perfectly marvelous day at school?

**DREW:** I had a perfectly marvelous day at school. Eighth grade is my beacon of happiness. *(Of the sign)* Is this good?

**MOTHER:** It's beautiful. Just don't cram everything over to the side.

**DREW:** You want it to say "Mom" or "Mother"?

**MOTHER** *(testing it)*: "Aren't you glad your *Mom* didn't do this to you. . . ." "Aren't you glad your *Mother* didn't do this— "Mother." Use "Mother."

**DREW:** 'Kay.

*(MOTHER exits. PHOEBE enters, carrying a saxophone case.)*

**DREW:** Hey. You left your socks on my bed this morning. They stink.

**PHOEBE:** What are you doing?

**DREW:** Making a sign, whatsit look like?

**PHOEBE:** Where's Mom?

**DREW:** Kitchen—

**PHOEBE:** Mom. . . ?

*(MOTHER enters.)*

**MOTHER:** Oh, you're home, dear, listen—

**PHOEBE:** —can I talk to you—?

**MOTHER:** See our signs? Now, we have to get an early start tomorrow.

**PHOEBE:** Mom, I can't, I have a test first period.

**MOTHER:** Oh— *(makes a raspberry)* —I'll write you an excuse.

**PHOEBE:** You wrote me an excuse *last* time, they're not going to take one this time.

**MOTHER:** We just need you for a few minutes. Just for when they open up. Soon as they open, you can take off.

**PHOEBE:** Look, all right, I have got to talk—

**MOTHER:** Oh, Drew! Look at that! You put the apostrophe in the wrong place!

**DREW:** What? A-R-E-apostrophe-N-T.

**PHOEBE:** It goes after the N.

**MOTHER:** That's right, good for you. *(Giggles.)* See? What do you need school for?

**DREW** *(of the sign)*: I don't think that's right—

**PHOEBE:** It goes after the N, who *cares*—

**MOTHER:** We will not have misspellings. We can't have misspellings—

**PHOEBE:** I have to—

**MOTHER:** —people think you're stupid when you misspell, all the texting? It's made you people *stupid*—

**PHOEBE:** Mom, *please*, I have to talk to you about something.

**MOTHER:** We come from a long line of spellers. Intelligent people. Your grandmother was a national champion.

**PHOEBE:** What are we, racehorses? Jesus Christ. . .

**MOTHER:** Well, aren't you *pleasant* today. *(To DREW)* Don't listen to her, Drew—

**PHOEBE:** (What else is new?)

13

**MOTHER:** —gets a burr under her saddle about *some*thing and *poof!* she's a snotnose.

**PHOEBE:** Okay, is Dad home?

**MOTHER:** No.  Just remember your brains, Drew.  Your common sense.  Don't ever try *not* to have sense about things.  That's no way to live.  Remember where you come from.  You have to remember . . .

**ALL THREE:** . . .where you come from to know where you're going.

*(DREW and the MOTHER laugh.  PHOEBE stands for a moment.)*

**DREW:** Remember. . . ?

**PHOEBE:** Very good, my sister. . .

**DREW:** . . .you must. . .

*(DREW stands.  The ENSEMBLE gathers around her, as STUDENTS in her high school classroom.)*

**PHOEBE:** . . .my baby sister all grown up. . .

*(The actress playing PHOEBE takes her place in the "classroom," now playing KELLY.)*

**DREW:** . . .you must remember where you've been. . .

**KELLY** *(under her breath)*: I know I'm gonna fail, 'cuz I been asleep this whole time.

*(Laughter from the other STUDENTS.)*

**DREW:** Kelly, I'd like to speak with you after class, okay?

**KELLY:** 'Kay.

**DREW:** So, all right.  Questions? And no cheating. If I see anyone searching on their phone, I'll collect it.

*(A student, JIMMY, raises his hand.)*

**JIMMY:** Yeah. Um. Okay. My topic is about civilian life in Germany during World War II.

**DREW:** That's good.

**JIMMY:** Yeah. Um. I. . .okay, I don't want to write about civilians. There's nothing exciting about them. It just talks about what they do every day. I wanna report on something else, like, like stars who joined the armies back then, like Errol Flynn—

**DREW:** Well. . .

**JIMMY:** —or *spies.*

**DREW:** Jimmy, let me ask you something: What would your life be like if you were alive during the war?

**JIMMY:** Same as always, prolly, bored as hell, prolly, like always.

*(Laughter from the class.)*

**DREW:** Ah. You didn't grow up in Afghanistan, so it doesn't count? You don't live in Charlottesville so you don't worry about it? It's just some video? Come on, now. You're part of this. Why? Because you're alive in the world. Now, think. Germany, it's 1943, what music do you hear on the radio? What voices? Where do you have to go to get soap? What are you paying attention to? *(Beat.)* What happens if you get caught playing somewhere you shouldn't? And I don't mean by your parents. I mean by someone *else. (Beat.)* What if your best friend is Jewish?

**JIMMY:** I don't know any Jewish people.

**DREW:** But what if you *did?* See? And what if they want you to hide them?

**JIMMY:** People get caught.

**DREW:** Yes. All of a sudden, things aren't so simple just because you're a civilian.

**A STUDENT:** Would you hide them?

*(FRANNIE, a pregnant woman, appears, gesturing toward DREW.)*

**FRANNIE:** Psst—!

**DREW:** That's. . .uh. . .you see, that's the thing, you have to make that decision on your own.

**A STUDENT:** Germany's okay now, so who cares?

**DREW:** Well. . .

**A STUDENT:** . . . but look at the Middle East—

**ANOTHER STUDENT:** —dude, North Korea—

**A STUDENT:** —'shwat I'm *saying*—

**YET ANOTHER STUDENT:** —Mother Russia, baby, *inside* job—

**DREW:** Well, it might be argued—

*(FRANNIE mouths: "I have to talk to you.")*

**A STUDENT:** —how they get so strong—

**DREW:** —that's *why* we look at Germany, especially, something called "the Phoenix Factor."

**KELLY** *(whispers to another student)*: Like in Arizona?

**THE STUDENT** *(whispers back to KELLY)*: *Jesus,* just go back to sleep, please—

**DREW:** The myth of the Phoenix bird is that, after it's destroyed, it rises from the ashes and becomes strong again, because it survived the worst that could happen.

**A STUDENT:** That's what I said, Germany is okay.

**DREW:** Sure, strength feels good, if you're the one getting stronger. But we've been walked right up to the annihilation line a couple of times in the last couple of years—

*(A bell is heard; the STUDENTS exit.)*

**DREW** *(as the students exit)*:  —all right, that's another discussion.  Reports in two weeks, if you run into trouble with your topics, come talk to me.  Remember, you *must* use at least one book as a source, a real book, paper pages and everything—

*(KELLY approaches DREW.)*

**KELLY:** You said you want to see me?

**DREW:** Yes, I did, I just wondered—

**KELLY:** —I know, I fell asleep, it's just, I have to take care of my brothers when I get home from school, they're jerks, I have to do my homework, I have to go to work, I don't get home till late, then Lou gets up at the crack of light, he's five, dog wants to pee so she's licking my face all over, Petey and John start fighting before they even wake *up*, I think, and— *(Pause.)* What?

**DREW** *(pause)*: Nothing.

**KELLY:** You're looking at me (hi, Ms. Sutton. . .)

**FRANNIE:** Hi, Kelly.

**KELLY:** . . .what are you looking at?

**MOTHER** *(appears to one side)*: How much did you know?

**DREW:** It's nothing, it's silly.  You look like someone.

**MOTHER**: I am insulted.  And she is dead.

*(FRANNIE clears her throat.)*

**KELLY:** I look like everybody.  I wish I had a, I don't know, I wish I had a face.  All right, I gotta go.  Bye Ms. Greer, bye Ms. Sutton. *(At FRANNIE's swollen middle.)* Bye Anna Regina!

**FRANNIE:** Oh, don't wake her up, she'll kick the hell out of me—

*(KELLY exits.)*

17

**DREW:** God, she's running herself ragged.

**FRANNIE:** Well, her mother isn't too. . .you ever met her?

**DREW:** Yeah. . .

**FRANNIE:**. . .it's only real bad when she breathes on you, all those different brands. Come on, we gotta get to the faculty meeting.

*(DREW makes a face.)*

**FRANNIE:** None a' that, girlfriend. You've been sent for.

**DREW:** What?

**FRANNIE:** "They're bootin' ya upstairs, kid. . ."

**DREW:** I don't—

**FRANNIE:** "You're goin' out a youngster, but you're coming back a star. . ."

**DREW:** *What?*

**FRANNIE** *(sudden change)***:** Got a pencil I could borrow?

**DREW:** What are you—?

**FRANNIE:** —Pen? Marker—?

**DREW:** —you better tell me—

**FRANNIE:** —quill and ink—?

**DREW:** *Frannie.*

**FRANNIE:** Yes? *(A jolt at her belly.)* Oh. Jesus. . .

**DREW:** See? Instant karma. That's what you get.

**FRANNIE** *(still feeling the twinge)***:** (. . .I think I fucked Jackie Chan, I just don't remember it. . .)

**DREW:** Here. Sit. Now, what?

**FRANNIE:** All right. Drew. Light of my life—

**DREW:** Would you just—!

**FRANNIE:** —you have been nominated for the State Board of Education.

**DREW:** Oh my God! *(Beat.)* You're kidding.

**FRANNIE:** Yes. I'm kidding. Actually, they nominated me. You thought Betsy was the end of the dumbing down. You had no idea.

**DREW:** (Shut up. . .)

**FRANNIE:** No, anyway, it's the truth, my love. *And* further, I am told you're the youngest ever to be so distinguished. Another reason for my alpha-bitch envy.

**DREW:** That's. . .that's incredible, I. . .I don't know if I'm ready for it.

**FRANNIE** *(struggles to her feet)***:** Oh, don't be such a pussy.

**DREW:** Frannie!

**FRANNIE:** Well, I'm sorry. What do you want, a parade too?

**MOTHER:** How much did you know?

**FRANNIE:** . . .you're ready, you're ready, things come when you're ready. . .

*(PHOEBE appears.)*

**PHOEBE:** Drew!

**FRANNIE:** You handle 'em because you have to handle 'em.

**PHOEBE:** Drew, you have to help me. . . !

**FRANNIE:** So let's go schmooze the shit out of them, whattaya say?

**DREW** *(beat; then)*: Sorry? Oh. . . *(Laughs a little.)* Too busy thinking. I'm concerned about Phoebe.

**FRANNIE:** Who?

**DREW:** What?

**FRANNIE:** Phoebe who?

**PHOEBE:** What am I gonna *do?*

**DREW:** What did I say? Phoebe?

**PHOEBE:** You have to help me, now wake *up.*

**DREW:** I meant Kelly.

**FRANNIE:** Hey, she's young, these are the Best Years of Her Life. If she can keep from getting knocked up by a kid with his ass hangin' out of his jeans, she'll be fine. Or shot by some maniac, Jesus.

**DREW** *(gentle teasing)*: And you wonder why you weren't nominated.

**FRANNIE:** Yeah, I'd *so* looked forward to subverting from within. Or at least getting a weekend on Betsy's yacht. Are we going, O Mighty Sarasvati, I gotta sit down pretty soon.

**DREW:** Frannie?

**FRANNIE:** Yeah?

**DREW:** How did you, I mean, the baby and all. How did you know you were. . . ?

**FRANNIE** *(shrugs)*: I looked in the mirror one morning and I couldn't stop smiling. I think, really, truly, for the first time in my life, I was smiling.

**DREW:** That's it? Smiling?

**FRANNIE:** That's it. That and the fact that I realized I hadn't seen schmucko for days or even had a text.

**FRANNIE** *(cont'd)***:** Men have some sort of radar for this stuff. I think they know before *we* do, they just don't want to say anything. And he was gone, gone, gone.

**DREW:** I'm sorry.

**FRANNIE:** Why? *You* didn't leave me. *(Pause.)* Y'know, if men could get pregnant—

**DREW:** —there'd be no war.

**FRANNIE:** Aw, you're cute. Actually, PMS would stand for pre-military strike.

*(They laugh; beat.)*

**DREW:** Are you scared?

**FRANNIE** *(pause)*: Look: I reached. . .inside my mind. I got down on my knees, in my mind, and I thanked God for all of it. *(Beat.)* Am I scared? Hell, yeah. And I can't wait.

**DREW** *(breathless)***:** Wow. . .this is happening, I can't believe this is all happening, what am I gonna do—?

**FRANNIE:** I'll tell you what you're *not* gonna do. You're not gonna fuck this up, that's what. Gird your loins, little Joanie D'Arc, let's go kick some Board of Ed ass, okay?

*(FRANNIE exits, laughing.)*

**DREW:** Shit. *(Pause.)* Oh, shit.

*(Music. The ENSEMBLE MEMBERS take up their positions for a funeral as a PREACHER'S voice is heard.)*

**PREACHER:** Friends
  We stand here
  In the sight of our God
  And commend the body
  Of our sister

**MOTHER:** daughter

**FATHER:** daughter

**DREW:** sister

**PHOEBE'S BOYFRIEND:** girlfriend

**3ᴿᴰ WOMAN:** friend

**DREW:** Oh, Phoebe. . .

*(PHOEBE's high, clear voice is heard as she emerges from the ENSEMBLE.)*

**PHOEBE** *(sings)*: I COULD BE THE PRESIDENT

**PREACHER:** terrible tragedy

**PHOEBE** *(sings)*: I COULD BE A FOOL

**3ᴿᴰ WOMAN:** whore

**2ᴺᴰ MAN:** got what was coming to her

**3ᴿᴰ WOMAN:** if you ask me

**PHOEBE** *(sings)*: I COULD MAKE A CRAZY WORLD

**PREACHER:** To the ground we send her body
  To heaven

**PHOEBE** *(sings)*: A LITTLE BETTER, WHO KNOWS

**3ᴿᴰ WOMAN:** to hell with her

**PREACHER:** Her soul takes flight, so
  Comfort her
  But think of us as well
  For we need comfort too

**PHOEBE** *(sings)*: THERE COULD BE ANOTHER MAN

**3ᴿᴰ WOMAN:** too young

**2ᴺᴰ MAN:** too *some*thing

**PHOEBE** *(sings)***:** I'LL STAY WITH HIM AND HE WITH ME

**3<sup>RD</sup> WOMAN:** too *loose*

**2<sup>ND</sup> MAN:** ssssh

**3<sup>RD</sup> WOMAN:** too loose by *half*

**PHOEBE** *(sings)***:** I WILL LIVE MY LIFE

**2<sup>ND</sup> MAN:** terrible tragedy

**3<sup>RD</sup> MAN:** ssssssh

**PREACHER:** Ashes to ashes
  Dust to dust
  Our daughter Phoebe
  Bury her we must

**PHOEBE** *(sings)***:** IT IS MINE!

**PREACHER:** We'll not judge, no
    *(His tone changes.)*
  But know ye the truth
  Locked in a toilet
  With a bottle of vermouth
  A Jezebel and not a Ruth
  Was Phoebe Greer
    *(Bringing himself under control.)*
  Glory comes when 'twill
  And judgment's near
  Draw you nigh
  We'll plant her here

**PHOEBE** *(sings)***:** IT IS MINE!

**PREACHER:** And we'll hope this

**2<sup>ND</sup> MAN:** Terrible tragedy

**PREACHER:** Soon passes from sight
  For it is not right
  That this child of night's

**PREACHER** *(cont'd)*: Pleasures should blight
   The One True Light
   Of our little community, for:
   We're All God-Fearing People Here

**PHOEBE** *(sings)*: I WILL BE A MILLION THINGS
   I AM MINE!
   I AM MINE!
   I AM—

**3<sup>RD</sup> WOMAN:** terrible tragedy, we're so sorry

**FATHER:** thank you

**MOTHER:** thanks and glory be

*(PHOEBE is silenced. The ENSEMBLE MEMBERS file past the MOTHER, the FATHER, and DREW.)*

**PREACHER:** if I can be of any

**2<sup>ND</sup> MAN:** tragedy

**3<sup>RD</sup> WOMAN:** I'll come over to the house, I'll bring

**PREACHER:** terrible tragedy

**3<sup>RD</sup> WOMAN:** a ham

**2<sup>ND</sup> MAN:** we can't stay long, of course

**MOTHER:** of course

**FATHER:** of course

**PREACHER** *(walking past the family)*: it's a terrible thing and are you all right?

*(The PREACHER, THE 2<sup>ND</sup> MAN, and the 3<sup>RD</sup> WOMAN exit. The MOTHER, FATHER and DREW stand. Silence.)*

**FATHER:** I'll get the car. *(Pause.)* Should I wait to get the car?

**MOTHER:** What?

**FATHER:** I mean, do we need more time here?

*(Silence.)*

**MOTHER:** No.  Don't worry.  We won't keep you.  Get the car.

**FATHER:** That's not what I (you always *do* this. . .)

**MOTHER:** Get the car, please.  Let's go home.  There are people coming over.

**FATHER:** We need to get some clean plates. *(Pause.)* There's nothing clean.  We need plates if there are people coming over.

**MOTHER:** Yes, all right.  We'll get the plates if you'll get the car.  Now is that all right?

*(Pause.  The FATHER exits.  Silence.)*

**MOTHER:** Flowers are pretty.

**DREW:** Yes.  Oh.  Oh, Mommy, *Jesus*. . .

*(DREW is crying; the MOTHER hugs her.)*

**MOTHER:** I know. . .

**DREW:** . . .Jesus *Christ*. . .

**MOTHER:** . . .sssh, love, don't talk like that here. . .

**DREW:** . . .it hurts, everything hurts, my stomach. . .

**MOTHER:** . . .ssh. . .

**DREW:** . . .we're going ice-skating, she *said*, she *said* we'd—to the movies, she stole my shirt. . .

**MOTHER:** . . .ssh. . .

**DREW:** . . .oh, God. . .

**MOTHER:** . . .ssh. . . *(Pause.)* We just. . .we have to know that she loved us all very much. *(Pause.)*

25

**MOTHER** *(cont'd)*: Somehow, she did what she did because she. . .loved us so much.  Isn't that right?

**DREW:** I don't know.

**MOTHER:** Oh, I think so.  I do.

*(Silence.)*

**DREW:** I promise, Mama. . .

**MOTHER:** . . .ssh. . .

**DREW:** . . .I promise. *(Pause.)* I won't die.

**MOTHER:** Everybody dies, baby.  It was Phoebe's time.

*(Silence.  DREW just looks at her MOTHER.)*

**MOTHER:** Yes.  God called her home, it was, it was—

**DREW:** Her time? *(Pause.)* Her *time?*  She's two years older than me, she's sixteen, how can it be her *time?*

*(Silence.)*

**MOTHER:** I don't know—

**DREW:** —it's not her *time*, that's *bullshit.*

**MOTHER:** Drew! *(Pause.)* You know better.
   You are fourteen years old, you are in a place of God's, you
      know better.
   It starts with your words.
   We all of us hurt, we're all of us grinding up inside.
   But, you must be careful.  You must be very careful, you
   must. . . .We're tested all the time, baby.  And we get
   stronger.  Now, don't we?  We just. . .we get. . .

*(The MOTHER weeps.)*

**DREW:** I'm sorry.

**MOTHER** *(a prayer)*: (Oh, *please.* . .)

**DREW:** Ssssh, Mama. . .

**MOTHER:** (. . .*please*. . .)

**DREW:** . . .ssssh. . .

**MOTHER:** All right.
All right.
No. Don't. You don't have to.
I am just fine.
I can fight, you know. I'm a fighter. A long line.

**DREW:** Yes, Mama. . .

**MOTHER:** . . .this this this this *pestilence*. We can *fight* it.
*(Silence; looks at DREW.)* What? *(Pause.)* What is it?

*(Silence. DREW shakes her head a little.)*

**DREW:** I'm sorry. *(Pause.)* And I promise.

**MOTHER:** All right.

**DREW:** I promise I won't hurt your feelings.

**MOTHER:** Just promise me that you'll come to me. That's all.
Just . . .there is nothing so bad it can't be fixed.

**DREW:** Yes, Mama.

**MOTHER:** We can get through. . . .Nothing is so terrible, just. . .
just come to me. *(Pause.)* Because I cannot bury another daughter.

*(The MOTHER exits.)*

**DREW** *(looking at PHOEBE)***:** Phoebe? *(Pause.)* Phoebe?

*(PHOEBE moves away. BOBBY enters, whistling. DREW turns to
see him enter.)*

**DREW:** How did you get in here?

**BOBBY** *(beat)***:** I opened the door.

**DREW:** Did you knock?

**BOBBY:** No, I just opened the door.

**DREW** *(pause)***:** Oh. I see. *(Pause.)* Your check bounced.

**BOBBY:** Shiiiiiiiit. I'm sorry. I get paid on Friday.

**DREW:** It's all right.

**BOBBY:** I'm really sor—

**DREW:** I said okay, I went to the bank, just give me a check or Venmo me by Friday.

*(Silence.)*

**BOBBY:** Well, gosh, Sheriff, how about if I just give you cash, can we fergit about this whole thang?

**DREW:** Don't be an asshole, all right? *I* went to my bank, *I* talked them out of their ridiculous fucking fee, it's fine and yes, if you'd like to give me cash instead, I certainly won't refuse it. (*Pause*). I didn't know you were coming over.

**BOBBY:** I texted you—

**DREW:** But you didn't *say*—

**BOBBY:** Jesus God, I'm sorry. *(Pause.)* Okay—?

**DREW:** —I mean, Bobby, you walk *in* here—

**BOBBY:** I said I was sorry.

**DREW:** This is my *place*, it's—

**BOBBY** *(pulls out his phone)***:** Look, I found a couple nice places, I think we should take a look at them.

**DREW:** Oh, *that's* sweet, isn't it. *(Catches herself. Beat.)* I'm sorry. Never mind.

**BOBBY:** No. I do mind.

**BOBBY** *(cont'd)***:** I thought we were going to look for a place together. *(Pause.)* What, you have plans?

**DREW:** Well, actually, I thought we could sit here and talk.

**BOBBY** *(sits, mumbles)***:** Okay. Not as much fun as looking for an apartment but, hey, sure, we can do this.

**DREW:** We have a problem.

**BOBBY:** I know we have a problem, I bounced a check—

**DREW:** Bobby—

**BOBBY:** —and you don't lock your door against, you know, thugs like me, I guess.

**DREW:** I think maybe I could be pregnant. *(Pause.)* I may very well be pregnant. *(Pause.)* I'm pregnant.

*(PHOEBE, nearby, begins to hum lightly.)*

**BOBBY:** You kidding?

**DREW:** No, I'm not—

*(BOBBY lets out a whoop of joy, scoops DREW into his arms. She laughs, in spite of herself.)*

**DREW:** Bobby—!

**BOBBY:** You are the most amazing thing!

**DREW:** —come on now—

**BOBBY:** Give me a great big ol' sloppy kiss on my nose!

**DREW:** Bobby, put me down, this isn't funny. .

*(BOBBY tries to hide his smile, puts DREW down.)*

**DREW:** I'm on the pill. How could this happen?

29

*(BOBBY poses like Superman, with hands on hips, feet widespread, announces:)*

**BOBBY:** Why, I don't know—

**DREW** *(giggling)*: All right, all right, stop that—

**BOBBY:** —might it be—Super-Sperm?!!

*(He picks her up, twirls her and dances around.)*

**DREW** *(yells)*: Stop, Bobby!

*(BOBBY puts her down.)*

**DREW:** I mean, geez, could you just, I mean. . .I'm kind of upset about this. *(Begins to cry.)* Oh geez, hormones already.

**BOBBY:** You're *upset*? *(Pause.)* Really.

**DREW:** Yes. I mean. . .I'm very tired.

**BOBBY:** Me too. *(Pause.)* I mean, goddamnit, I am tired too, *how* many years have we been together?
I'm tired of having my clothes spread out over two apartments.
I'm tired of playing house, okay?
I thought we were going to do this, I would have thought. . .
*(Pause.)* We just need a bigger place right?

**DREW:** Oh, come *on*—

**BOBBY:** It would be cheaper than two rents.

**DREW:** I'm still paying off my school loans, and you—

*(Silence.)*

**BOBBY:** Drew, I bounced a check. You never bounced a check—?

**DREW:** I don't know if I can handle—God, or even *want* a child right now. *(Silence.)* I was just nominated for the Board of Ed today, and—

**BOBBY:** And what? They're going to kick you off if they find out you're pregnant?

**DREW:** No, but—

**BOBBY:** Why don't we just go, we'll walk, we'll look at these places—

**DREW:** *Bobby.* I'm not going anywhere, I'm not looking for a "place." I'm going to stay here, I need some, some *peace* with this. Please help me. Please. Okay?

**BOBBY:** I'll call you if I find something.

*(BOBBY exits. FRANNIE appears, holding her enormous belly.)*

**FRANNIE:** Go figure. I realized I hadn't seen schmucko for days, and I'm scared to death and I can't wait and I feel better and better and I'm scared to death and where is schmucko and oh, my, my, my, I am *smiling*. . .

**DREW:** Mama. . . ?

**FRANNIE:** . . .and I am pregnant. . .

**DREW:** . . .I'm home!

**FRANNIE:** . . .and in my mind, I thank my God. . . .

*(FRANNIE'S line is overlapped by the sound of a ticking clock as the MOTHER is discovered sitting in a rocking chair, staring front. She is not rocking.)*

**DREW:** What time is it? I was afraid I was late from school. What time is it? *(Pause.)* Mama—?

**MOTHER:** I don't know.

**DREW** *(pause)*: School was good today. I did good, teacher said—

**MOTHER:** It is the six-month anniversary of my daughter's death.
And I don't know where her father is.
I'll believe the best of him, very well.

**MOTHER** *(cont'd)*: He is at the cemetery.
  Why, you may ask, did he not ask me to go along?
  He wished to spare me my pain.
  Why, you may ask, did he take the last twenty-dollar bill
    from my purse?
  I'll believe the best of him, very well.
  He wished to buy her flowers.
  Why, you may ask, will he smell of wine and not roses when
    he returns? *(Perhaps chuckles at the allusion.)* I'll believe
    the best of him.
  He is not so strong as I and so he needs. . .hm. *(Pause.)*
  You see?
  Easier every day.

*(Silence.)*

**DREW:** I met a boy.

*(BOBBY appears off to the side, much younger.)*

**BOBBY:** I want to make one thing very clear: I do not carry
books.

**DREW** *(to BOBBY, laughing)*: Oh, yeah?

**MOTHER:** Oh, really?

**DREW** *(to the MOTHER)*: Yes.

**MOTHER:** What does he look like?

**DREW:** Very tall. I mean, taller than me anyway.

**MOTHER:** Mm. *(Pause.)* Your father was tall once.

**DREW** *(pause)*: Well, I'll just go upstairs.

**MOTHER:** Now, what does that mean—?

**DREW:** I'm just going to dust in the room—

**MOTHER:** —you "have met a boy"?

**DREW** *(pause)*: Yes.

32

**BOBBY:** What?

**DREW** *(to BOBBY)***:** I can't. That's all. I can't go.

**BOBBY:** It's a movie. You can't even go to a movie? An afternoon movie?

**DREW** *(to the MOTHER)***:** Mother, *please*?

**MOTHER:** . . .well, I need to know what that means.

**BOBBY:** We'll leave a seat between us.

**DREW:** It doesn't mean anything, I just said I—

**MOTHER:** Is he nice?

**DREW:** Yes.

**BOBBY:** I'm a nice guy. Ask anybody. It's disgusting, I have no *fun*. . .

**MOTHER:** Is he nice. . . ?

**DREW:** Of course he's nice.

**MOTHER:** . . .or is he just sniffing around. . . ?

**DREW** and **BOBBY:** *What*?

**MOTHER:** . . .because he's heard about the women in this family?

**DREW:** Don't talk about her that way.

**BOBBY:** I really think this could be the start of something wonderful. I memorized that from somewhere. What do you think?

**DREW** *(to BOBBY; laughs)***:** Jerk. I'll try. I mean. . .I want to, I just, I may have to do some things at home.

**BOBBY:** All *day*—?

**MOTHER:** She was my daughter.

33

**DREW:** I know, and she was my sister, so you don't say things like that.

**BOBBY:** Okay, look, then, I'm just going to ask you this: What about prom?

**MOTHER:** And I'm just going to ask you this: Will I lose you too?

**DREW:** Oh, Mama. . .

**MOTHER:** Will I quietly close the lid over your body?

**DREW:** Mama, come *on*. . .

**MOTHER:** Will you become like her—?

**DREW:** Don't *talk* about her like that. I'm not becoming anything, that's the *problem*, I'm *nothing*, I just said that I met a *boy*.

**MOTHER:** Oh, yes. That's how it begins for virtually everyone.

**DREW** *(to BOBBY)*: Look, I don't know. I want to. I want to. I really do. Now, please. . .

*(DREW impulsively kisses BOBBY's cheek. BOBBY exits.)*

**MOTHER:** I'll believe the best of you, very well.

**DREW:** *What*?

**MOTHER:** Why, then, did you never come to me with what you knew?

**DREW:** You're going crazy.

**MOTHER:** I'll believe the best of you. . .

**DREW:** You're driving yourself crazy, you know that, and people are *laughing* at us.

**MOTHER:** . . .you wished to spare me my humiliation.

**DREW:** Do you know what it's like for *me?*

**MOTHER:** Why, then, did you not come to me for advice?  For counsel?  For prayer?

**DREW:** Mama, please. . .

**MOTHER:** I will believe the best of you:  You felt you were being loyal, do you see?  To your sister who now lies in the earth for her sins. . .

**DREW:** Why are you doing this?

**MOTHER:** Because I want you to *remember.*

**PHOEBE** *(calling from the darkness)*:  Come!  Now!  Fast!

**DREW:** I didn't do anything wrong!

**MOTHER:** I will not bury another daughter.

**PHOEBE:** Come *on!*

**DREW** *(to PHOEBE)*:  What?

**MOTHER:** I will believe the best of you.

**PHOEBE:** You have to help me!

**MOTHER** *(to DREW)*:  I will. . .

**PHOEBE:** . . .*please.* . .

**MOTHER:** . . .but, what of *them?*  Those boys who want us to make them into *men?*  Eh?  What are we to think of *them?*

*(BOBBY is discovered talking to the FATHER.  Silence.)*

**FATHER:** You're sure.
  Now, you're sure.
  I mean, you're sure of what you've done to my daughter.

*(Silence.)*

**BOBBY:** Yes. I mean, *she's* sure. And I don't know why we can't just. . . *(Pause.)* I mean, we're *grownups.* What is this supposed to mean for people who are grownups?

**FATHER:** You know, I don't know. *(Pause.)* Did you want another beer?

**BOBBY:** Yes, please.

**FATHER:** Oh! Wait a second! Here. *(Produces two cigars.)* Here we are. How about this. This is. . .this is what we do, eh?

**BOBBY:** Well, actually, I think. . .

**FATHER:** Eh? What the hell.

*(They hold their cigars, not lighting them.)*

**FATHER:** I. . .I never. . .well, we all have our, what, our war-stories, *I* don't know.

**BOBBY:** *You* don't know. *(Pause.)* *I* sure don't know. *(Pause.)* I stalked out of her apartment. Geez.

**FATHER:** Huh.. .well, heh. . . .This was many years ago, of course.

**BOBBY:** Ah.

**FATHER:** After this party. *(Pause.)* It was just a game. That's all, just a, it didn't *mean* anything. *(Pause.)* And I *know* that.

**BOBBY:** Yes. *(Pause.)* What are you talking about?

**FATHER:** I don't know. *(Beat.)* I was at this party. And I'd told a coupla the fellows. Just. . .that, you know. . . . *(Long pause.)* Well, that Drew's mother was pregnant. With Phoebe, with our first. . .

**BOBBY:** . . .yes. . .

**FATHER:** . . .she's gone now. . .

**BOBBY:** . . .yes.

*(Pause. The FATHER raises his beer, in a sort of toast.)*

**FATHER:** Anyway. This game. Somebody took and put, *I* don't know, they stuck this plunger, you know, that you clean toilets with, *I* don't know, somebody stuck this plunger to the ceiling.

*(Silence.)*

**BOBBY:** What kind of game is that?

**FATHER:** I don't know. *(Pause.)* But they were. . .taking turns, these fellows. They would lay on the floor, and spread their legs, and wait for the plunger to drop to the floor, and if you could lay there and the plunger would *drop*, pointy end down, and, you know, *stabs* the floor between your legs. . . . *(Laughs a little.)* Well, you too could be a Man of the Hour.

**BOBBY:** Mmm.

**FATHER:** Now, Sal and Alex, they had invented this game, so, of course, they laid down there and the plunger drops, right between their legs, but *close*, y'know what I mean, I mean *close*. Like they coulda lost their *balls*, they weren't careful. But they laid there like fucking *stone*, that fuckin thing *stabs* the floor between their legs. *(Pause.)* And everybody holds their breath for a second, can't believe it. And then the room *erupts*. Everybody applauding. And all the *guys*, they light a *cigar*, and everybody claps 'em on the *back*, and. . .well.

**BOBBY:** You laid on the floor.

**FATHER:** How could I *not*? *(Beat.)* See, I had told Sal and Alex that she was pregnant, see, which, of course, they didn't say anything. Like, they didn't believe me. *(Pause.)* I mean, how could *I*? *(Pause.)* You know what I mean, I mean, how could *I* get anybody . . . in that way? Like a father. . . . .Like a *man*, how could I be a man, some *stud*. . . in that way.

**BOBBY:** Mmm.

**FATHER:** So I'm laying there. I'm hearing "Dad-*dy*, Dad-*dy*, Dad-*dy*," I'm looking up't the ceiling—

**FATHER** *(cont'd)*: —and here's this plunger just ready to drop, right on my balls (or *some*where). . .and I feel my balls *freeze.* "Dad-*dy*, Dad-*dy*, Dad-*dy*. . ." *(Silence.)* Perhaps it's that it's the first time you hear the word, perhaps that's what does it to you. That thing dropped off the ceiling. . .I folded up like a flower on a cloudy day. Plunger dropped off the side of my leg. Hardly even felt it. And the whole room got quiet. And two seconds later everybody is laughing. *(Pause.)* A couple people clapped, though. *(Pause.)* I'm a good sport. They all say so.

**BOBBY:** I would say so.

**FATHER:** Thank you. Little later, everybody lit up cigars. *(Pause.)* I hate cigars. God*damn*, I wanted one. You see?

**BOBBY:** Mmm.

**FATHER:** They were very nice about it, understand. *(Pause.)* Everybody clapped me on the back. At least, they said, I was *out there.* Plenty a guys never even *laid* on the floor, for*get* it. *(Pause.)* A couple of the women came up, told me they thought it was a silly game. I agreed. So all the fellows lit up their cigars, and guess what? They gave me one. And we stood there, the. . .guys and me. *(Pause.)* I excused myself from the party. And I walked. Puffing on my cigar.

*(PHOEBE is discovered reading an email on her phone. DREW stands and watches.)*

**PHOEBE** *(reading)*: And I know

*(PHOEBE'S BOYFRIEND appears from the darkness.)*

**PHOEBE'S BOYFRIEND:** you will understand why I've left, and I know you will understand that I haven't left *you*, really. . .

**FATHER:** And with cigar on my breath and
  A song in my heart
  I took the bull by the well-worn horns
  Walked over to her house and
  Con*vinced* her to marry me. Huh.

38

*(Silence.)*

**FATHER:** Is this helping you at all?

*(BOBBY shakes his head.)*

**PHOEBE'S BOYFRIEND:** And I know. . .

**FATHER:** Well, then. . .

**PHOEBE'S BOYFRIEND:** . . .well, I *hope*

**PHOEBE** *(reading)*: someday we can be together again, maybe

**FATHER:** . . .you need another beer?

**BOBBY:** No, I don't think so.

**FATHER:** Awww, c'mah. . . . *(Pause; nods.)* Nope.  Nope.
Don't blame you one little bit. *(Of the cigar.)* Now, you save
that for later.

**BOBBY:** Thank you.

**FATHER:** I make no excuses.

**BOBBY:** No.

**FATHER:** I chose, to do it.
   I laid on the floor.
   For my *life*.
   With her.

**BOBBY:** Yes.

**FATHER:** I *stayed*.

**BOBBY:** That's right.

**PHOEBE'S BOYFRIEND:** And I know

**PHOEBE** *(reading)*: you will forgive me, baby

**FATHER** *(makes sound and gesture, as of plunger falling; then)*: Plenty a guys never. . . *(Beat.)*
  Huh. *(Beat.)*
  I rolled over at perhaps a crucial moment, but . . . *(Sighs.)*
  No regrets. That's the important thing. *(Beat.)*
  In, what. . .in *life*. *(Beat.)*
  I *stayed*. *(Beat.)*
  By and large and in the main, I *stayed*.

**PHOEBE** *(reading)* and **HER BOYFRIEND**: Baby, I am so sorry.

*(Silence. DREW is near PHOEBE, listening.)*

**DREW**: Is that from Kevin?  Who is that from?

**PHOEBE**: Nobody.

**PHOEBE'S BOYFRIEND**: Baby, I

**PHOEBE** *(softly mimicking)*: Baby, I

**PHOEBE'S BOYFRIEND**: Baby, it's

**PHOEBE**: Baby, it's

**PHOEBE'S BOYFRIEND**: Baby, I

**PHOEBE**: Baby, I had a great time, but it's late, shouldn't we
    be getting you home?
  Baby, "good night?"  Why, it's early yet, why don't you come
    to my house for awhile?
  Baby, didn't you have a nice time?
  Baby, then do you wanna come in?
  Baby, it's late.
    Baby, you know, it's late.
    Baby, you know, it's late, do you wanna just stay here for
    the night?
  Baby, call em, tell em you're staying with a friend

**DREW**: What?

**PHOEBE**: Tell her I'm staying with a friend

40

**DREW:** *What* friend?

**PHOEBE:** *I* don't know.  Jessica.

*(JESSICA is revealed on her phone.)*

**JESSICA:** Hi, Phoeble!

**DREW:** She's staying with a friend. . .

**MOTHER:** *What* friend?

**DREW:** Jessica.

**JESSICA:** Oh, *Drew.*  God, you and Phoeble sound just alike. . .

**MOTHER:** Jessica who?

**DREW:** Oh, Mama, who knows?  Can I have something to eat?

**MOTHER and PHOEBE'S BOYFRIEND:** Baby, it's so late

**JESSICA:** Geez, it's so late.  Okay, so she's supposed to be staying here tonight.  But tell her she owes me one.

*(JESSICA disappears.)*

**PHOEBE** *(mimicking)***:** Baby, baby, baby, it's so late is it all right if I kiss you?

**FATHER:** It's late.  Where the hell is she?

**MOTHER:** Staying with a friend.  Do you want something to eat?

**PHOEBE and HER BOYFRIEND:** Baby, you can lay down here.

**PHOEBE:** Baby, do you mind?

**PHOEBE'S BOYFRIEND:** I can't sleep if I have em on.
  Baby

**PHOEBE:** are you really comfortable in those?
  Baby, you are so beautiful.
  Baby, I think I could

**PHOEBE'S BOYFRIEND:** maybe someday possibly be

**PHOEBE:** in love with you
  Baby, does that feel

**PHOEBE'S BOYFRIEND:** good?
  Baby, I am so sorry

**PHOEBE:** that I haven't called you

*(Lights up on JESSICA.)*

**JESSICA:** What *happened*?

**PHOEBE:** Baby, it's just a couple of days late

**PHOEBE'S BOYFRIEND:** Baby

**PHOEBE:** I wouldn't worry

**JESSICA:** I wouldn't worry. . .

**PHOEBE:** Baby, could you go to the doctor and see

**PHOEBE'S BOYFRIEND:** I can't sleep nights I worry so much.

**JESSICA:** I could call the doctors. . .

**PHOEBE'S BOYFRIEND:** Whatta you *mean* you got two lines?

**PHOEBE:** Baby, whatta we gonna do?

**PHOEBE'S BOYFRIEND:** Baby

**PHOEBE:** I can't stand this pressure, what am I gonna do?

**PHOEBE'S BOYFRIEND:** Baby

**PHOEBE:** what can I possibly ever in this big bad ole world we live in *do*?

**PHOEBE'S BOYFRIEND:** Baby, I can't

**PHOEBE:** Baby, I can't

**PHOEBE'S BOYFRIEND:** Baby, I

**PHOEBE:** Baby, I
 Baby, I, I, I, *I!*

**PHOEBE'S BOYFRIEND:** Baby, I've talked to lots of people

**JESSICA:** He came to me, I guess he just wanted to talk

**PHOEBE:** And it's not so bad

**JESSICA:** Nothing *happened*, we were looking on the Internet, now—

**PHOEBE:** Baby, it just hurts a little

**PHOEBE'S BOYFRIEND:** And it's not so bad

**JESSICA:** You're paranoid nothing *happened* and this is what I told him:

**PHOEBE'S BOYFRIEND:** And it's not so bad

**JESSICA and PHOEBE'S BOYFRIEND:** hurts a little

**PHOEBE'S BOYFRIEND:** come on

**PHOEBE:** It—just be a big ol' girl about this—

**PHOEBE and HER BOYFRIEND:** hurts a *little*

**PHOEBE'S BOYFRIEND:** Baby, I am so *sorry.*

*(PHOEBE'S BOYFRIEND disappears.)*

**JESSICA:** I'll help. Yes, he e-mailed me, it was a *courtesy*, for god's sake, stop being so paranoid. . .

**PHOEBE** *(to DREW)***:** I want you to shut your mouth about this.

**DREW:** Okay.

**PHOEBE:** I'm trusting you with this thing. If you open your mouth about it. . .

**DREW:** . . .I won't—

**PHOEBE:** —I'll kill you.  And I'll hate your guts till the day I die.

**DREW:** Okay.  I won't say anything.

**PHOEBE:** And will you help me?

**DREW:** How?

**PHOEBE:** I am asking you a question.

**DREW:** Help you do what?

**PHOEBE:** I don't trust Jessica. . .

**JESSICA:** . . .Phoeble, I can't make anything out of this, it's too much, yes, he texts me, for God's sake, nothing much is going on at *all*, will you *stop*?  Good luck.

*(JESSICA disappears.)*

**PHOEBE:** . . .so will you help me do whatever it is I'm going to do?

**DREW:** I'm your sister.

**PHOEBE** *(pause)***:** So, what now?

*(Silence.)*

**DREW:** Where is he?

**PHOEBE** *(of the letter)***:** Doesn't say.

**DREW:** Maybe he'll come back.

*(Silence, as PHOEBE looks at DREW.)*

**DREW:** What about. . .

*(Silence.)*

**PHOEBE:** What about what?

**DREW:** You're not going to. . .

**PHOEBE:** I haven't got the slightest idea what you're talking about, Drew.

**DREW:** Well, you're going to have it, aren't you?

**PHOEBE** *(beat)*: What are you talking about?
    *DO I LOOK LIKE I'M GOING TO HAVE IT?!*
    *WHAT ARE YOU FUCKING TALKING ABOUT?!*

*(Silence. PHOEBE puts her head in her hands, and begins to sob quietly.)*

**PHOEBE:** I mean. . .I just

**BOBBY:** don't know, I just

**FATHER:** I don't know

**DREW:** I don't know how

**PHOEBE, FATHER, BOBBY** and **DREW:** *I just don't know how this happened.*

*(A whistle blast.)*

**3<sup>RD</sup> WOMAN:** Class!

**BOBBY:** I don't know what it means, I mean—

**3<sup>RD</sup> WOMAN:** Class!

**BOBBY:** —where do we *assimilate* this shit from?

**3<sup>RD</sup> WOMAN:** Class! Attention!

*(DREW and the ENSEMBLE MEMBERS stand at attention, as though in a barracks.)*

**3<sup>RD</sup> WOMAN:** Today we are going to talk about the Human Reproductive System.

*(The ENSEMBLE MEMBERS snicker.)*

**BOBBY** *(whispering)*: The what?

**2ᴺᴰ MAN:** She's talking about *fucking*, idiot.

*(The 3ᴿᴰ WOMAN, as a TEACHER, uses a pointer, pointing at various spots around her. The speech is done fast, with accompanying gestures, resembling a ground-to-air traffic controller.)*

**TEACHER:** Human life is a very precious thing and today we will see how that life, the miracle of life, is begun:

Since Adam named the first animal, my friends, things have been given names and it is no different here. You will hear several terms here today. Please consider these terms the *only* acceptable terms for these parts and processes, no matter *what* you hear on social media.

In addition, please be prepared to locate each of the so-named parts in your textbook. Every one of you has been given genitalia. Please locate the textbook plate labeled "genitalia."

**A VOICE** *(ala a game show host)*: The word is. . . "genitalia."

*(ENSEMBLE MEMBERS reach down and touch areas on the floor, as though in their "textbooks." Each time the TEACHER mentions a body part, the ENSEMBLE MEMBERS reach to a different point, resembling a game of "Twister." They may during the course of the lecture, touch each other—which they enjoy.)*

**TEACHER:** . . .and it is through that genitalia, which, incidentally, of course, as you know, is also responsible for the excretion of other bodily fluids in the male, the two systems are related. . .

**DREW:** What does *that* mean?

**2ᴺᴰ MAN:** We can pee, we can come, but we can't pee *and* come.

**TEACHER:** . . .a process known as "ejaculation". . .

**THE VOICE:** ". . .Ejaculation. . ."

**TEACHER:** . . .that the miracle of life is begun.

**TEACHER** *(cont'd)*: Please find "Life" in your textbook.

*(The ENSEMBLE MEMBERS momentarily stall.)*

**TEACHER:** Going on. . .

**PHOEBE** *(whispering to her classmates)*: . . .I've never known anything like it. . .

**TEACHER:** Miss Phoebe Greer, are you daydreaming again, *what are you thinking of*?

**MOTHER** *(pausing in the game)*: What Are You Thinking Of?

**TEACHER:** . . .when this genitalia contact in the accepted and completely natural insertive manner, which is only possible via passage through the external female genitalia collectively called the vulva. . .

**THE VOICE:** ". . .Vulva. . ."

*(BOBBY tries to find a place to "land" in the Twister game.)*

**BOBBY:** The *what*. . .?

**TEACHER:** . . .bounded by two folds of skin that enclose the vestibule. . .

**THE VOICE:** ". . .Vestibule. . ."

**BOBBY:** What's that?

**2ND MAN:** Like in church.

**DREW:** Mama, I heard something strange at school today, something about how a man—

**FATHER:** Hm?

**MOTHER**: You don't need to know about that.

**PHOEBE:** Well, what happens is

**2ND MAN:** My Mom said

**BOBBY:** My Dad wouldn't lie to me

**DREW:** I don't care, it's still crap, it's squishy like that, how are you going to get it *in* there?

**BOBBY:** you don't always have to, you know what my Dad said

**2<sup>ND</sup> MAN:** you can get her pregnant if she walks by in a bathing suit and you got a woodie

**THE VOICE:** ". . .Woodie. . ."

**TEACHER** *(sternly bringing the students back to the game)*: . . .the engorging of the penile erectile tissue. . .

**BOBBY:** yeah, it gets into the *air*

**2<sup>ND</sup> MAN:** like the 'rona, swear to God

**DREW:** a man puts his his his *thing*

**MOTHER**: Don't You Say "Thing" In This House!

**THE VOICE** *(whispers)*: ". . .Thing. . ."

*(Now PHOEBE gently and easily disengages herself from the Twister game.)*

**PHOEBE:** . . .well, what *do* you call it. . . ?

**MOTHER**: You Don't Need To Know About That.

**FATHER:** and, of course, well, you have to be married

**2<sup>ND</sup> MAN:** you have to be married

**FATHER:** before it will work

**2<sup>ND</sup> MAN:** or your babies will have tails like pigs

**BOBBY:** the guy lays on top of the girl

**2<sup>ND</sup> MAN** *(holds his phone)*: look here—

**DREW:** what—?

**2<sup>ND</sup> MAN:** —look at this. . .

**THE VOICE:** Oooooh!

**2<sup>ND</sup> MAN:** . . .now, does that look like he's on *top?*

**DREW:** Well, then *tell* me

**BOBBY:** *tell* me

**PHOEBE:** *tell* me

**TEACHER:** *Class, Are You Listening?* To continue: . . .into the properly lubricated vaginal cavity (where there is the release of seminal fluid) which may or may not contain an egg which begins to deteriorate about twelve hours maximum twenty-four hours after ovulation and can no longer be fertilized after that time unless consecrated by a prayer to Saint Jude on the Tuesday before Christmas, or the end of Holiday Gift Specials, whichever comes first. . .

**BOBBY:** What does that mean?

**2<sup>ND</sup> MAN:** She can't get pregnant the first time you fuck her.

**FATHER:** Tell you what, for heaven's sake, there's no big mystery about it. . .

**PHOEBE:** Oh yes, there most assuredly is.

**MOTHER:** It is *Sacred* Mystery

**FATHER:** simple biological function

**MOTHER:** which is how it must remain

**2<sup>ND</sup> MAN:** the guy lays on top of the girl

**BOBBY** *(confidently)***:** yup

**PHOEBE:** oh yes

**BOBBY:** they rub a lot

**DREW:** and their belly buttons snap together to make a baby. But you have to have an innie and an outie for it to work.

**FATHER:** nothing to it

**PHOEBE:** his hardness, his heat, my warmth and wetness, my

**FATHER:** whatdoyoucallit, the uh, the uh, the uh—

**MOTHER**: What are you *telling* her??

**FATHER:** —what time is it?

**DREW:** Why do you keep asking that?

**MOTHER**: You Don't Need To Know—

**DREW:** —but—

**MOTHER**: *You Don't Need To Know About That!*

**DREW:** Why *not*?!

**MOTHER**: Because *Sex Is BEAUTIFUL!*

*(Music oozes into the space: a sleazy saxophone. The 3ʳᵈ
WOMAN suddenly abandons her "Teacher" persona, and
retrieves a cell phone from her bra.)*

**3ᴿᴰ WOMAN** *(on the phone, at the MOTHER)*: Are you tired of
being lonely?

*(MOTHER looks confused.)*

**MOTHER**: That is. . .it's it's it's *natural.*

**3ᴿᴰ WOMAN**: Wanna hear my confessions?

**MOTHER** *(looking ill)*: Just like a heart attack.

**3ᴿᴰ WOMAN**: Find that special someone?
  Make a confession of your own *to* that special someone?
  Well, all you need to do
  Is call me

**BOBBY:** Tell me

**3<sup>RD</sup> WOMAN:** Call me

**DREW:** Text me

**3<sup>RD</sup> WOMAN:** Call me

**PHOEBE:** Skype me

*(The 3<sup>RD</sup> WOMAN hides the cell phone in her bra, blows her whistle, and instantly resumes her "Teacher" persona.)*

**TEACHER:** *Class! Please keep your attention properly focused!*
To continue: . . .which means fertilization can occur only when sperm is present in the upper third of the oviduct during the 12 to 24 hours immediately following ovulation with conception not possible during the other 27 days of a 28 day cycle. . . .

**BOBBY:** So, *when* could she get pregnant?

**2<sup>ND</sup> MAN:** Look, just use a rubber. If it breaks on a bad day, leave town.

**TEACHER:** And it is indeed

**PHOEBE:** A miracle
   A miracle
   I took him into my body
   Into the very core of me
   And it could not have been a sin
   How was it a wrong
   How could it have been anything but
   The most amazing thing in the world?

**TEACHER:** And it is indeed
   As you can see, the most
   Natural
   Beautiful
   Ecstatic
   Thing in the world. *(Beat.)*
   Just don't do it yet.

**MOTHER:** Just come to me

**3ᴿᴰ WOMAN:** Call me

**DREW** *(to BOBBY)***:** Text me

**3ᴿᴰ WOMAN:** Ping me

**BOBBY** *(to DREW)***:** Text me

**MOTHER:** Come to me. . .

**FATHER:** . . .sure, you can come to me, why not?

*(There is knocking.)*

**DREW:** Come in.

**3ᴿᴰ WOMAN:** Why not FaceTime me?

*(The ENSEMBLE MEMBERS are drifting away into shadow. DREW stands alone.)*

**DREW:** Come in.

*(Pause. A baby stroller is pushed onstage; it rolls gently to center. DREW looks at it. Pause. BOBBY pokes his head in.)*

**BOBBY:** There. I knocked. Better?

**DREW** *(smiling)***:** Thank you.

**BOBBY** *(hands her an envelope)***:** It's all there. So you don't have to break my legs.

**DREW** *(still smiling)***:** Thank you, again.

**BOBBY** *(referring to stroller)***:** Did you lose that? I found it outside, thought maybe we could, you know, use it. . .

**DREW:** What is this?

**BOBBY:** . . .do the whole marriage and family thing. . . . 'Course, we could always just sell it for parts, *I* don't know.

**DREW:** Bobby—

**BOBBY:** All right, listen, I found a place—please, just listen, okay—

**DREW:** I am, I'm listening, I'm—

**BOBBY** *(pulls out cell phone):* —it's nice, it's plenty big enough. *(Shows her pictures of the listing.)* From the baby's room, you can see the lake, it's— *(Beat.)* What?

**DREW:** My Dad called. He wants us to come over for dinner tonight.

**BOBBY:** Oh. Well. That's fine. . .yes?

**DREW:** You've got to be kidding.

**BOBBY:** You're just —

**DREW:** —I'm just paranoid, thank you, I know. *(Pause.)* Bobby, I can't sit down at the table with them.

**BOBBY** *(holding her):* It's dinner, that's all—

**DREW:** —oh *please*, do not try to talk to me like I'm on a ledge, okay? I don't know what I'm going to say to her.

**BOBBY:** So don't tell her.

**MOTHER** *(off):* Come to me. . .

**DREW:** Right. Bobby, she'll see through me like I'm a window. It's different between us. Not like when I was a kid. Back then, I could lie.

**BOBBY:** All right, then tell her. Tell them both.

**DREW:** Oh, sure. Their oh-so-respectable perfect little girl of twenty-four got herself knocked up—

**BOBBY:** (Gee, thanks.)

**DREW:** —and thinks. . .

*(Silence.)*

**Bobby:** What?

*(Silence. Drew goes to the stroller and looks at it for a long moment.)*

**Drew:** Bobby, I don't know—

**Bobby:** Don't—

**Drew:** What?  I need to talk to you before—

**Bobby:** Don't say it.  Things will work out and I don't want to hear otherwise or I swear to God, I'll. . .

**Drew** *(beat; calmly)*: You'll what, Bobby?

*(Silence.)*

**Bobby:** I. . .I just. . .I love you so much.  I love us together so much—

**Drew:** Then act like it.

**Bobby:** *What the hell do you think this is?*  I'm *here*.  I'm *proud* of that.  And now we have this, this, this chance to be this. . .awesome . . .storybook thing. . .

**Drew:** (. . .stories. . .)

**Mother:** . . .just promise. . .

**Drew:** (. . .and who knows what's true anymore. . .)

*(Bobby places Drew's hand on her belly.)*

**Bobby:** Feel that.  Feel what we've started up in there.  This baby wants to be born.  It beat the pill.

**Drew:** Oh, Bobby—

**Bobby:** —that's *the* truth—

**DREW:** Bobby, I—

**PHOEBE** *(off)*: There's a bus!

**DREW:** Bobby, before we go over there, I need to—

**PHOEBE:** I have to go—

**DREW:** —don't hate me—

**PHOEBE:** Come on!

**BOBBY:** Hate you? No, no, on the contrary, I have given you every blessing I know how to give, I'm *here*—

**PHOEBE:** It's me.

**BOBBY:** It isn't me.

**MOTHER:** Come to me.

**DREW:** But—

**BOBBY** *(disappointment, not an attack)*: God help us both, you're a coward.

**DREW** *(a disbelieving gasp)*: What?!

**PHOEBE:** Come *on*!

**BOBBY:** It isn't me, it's *you.*

**DREW:** You son of a *bitch—!*

**PHOEBE:** *Come on!*

**DREW** *(to PHOEBE)*: What?

**PHOEBE:** We have to go, there's the bus!

**DREW** *(to PHOEBE)*: What if they find out?

**BOBBY:** That's right, damn *me* to hell, fine—

**PHOEBE:** They won't find out—

**BOBBY:** —you're a goddamn coward, you'd rather sneak off and destroy everything—

**PHOEBE:** —I covered us at school, but we have to *go*—

**BOBBY:** —*everything*, rather than face her. That's what I think.

**DREW:** Oh my God—

**BOBBY:** You *selfish* coward.

**DREW** *(generally)***:** Oh my God, help me.

**BOBBY:** And now we'll all sit down to dinner—

**DREW:** How *dare* you say to me—

**PHOEBE:** *We have to go!*

**DREW:** I can't do this!

**PHOEBE:** *YOU'VE GOT TO HELP ME NOW!*

**DREW** *(to PHOEBE)***:** *ALL RIGHT! (Pause.)* All *right.*

*(DREW looks at PHOEBE who reaches for DREW. Blackout.)*

### End Act One

# *Act Two*

## ACT TWO

*(The stage is darkened. A low light rises showing DREW in the same spot as at the end of Act One.)*

**DREW:** When I was a little girl, I saw that my sister had become much older with the setting of one sun.

When I was a little girl, I heard that I was to grow up too, and quickly, because there were lives in the balance.

When I grew up, I saw that blood would not stay put but spread to the corners and pooled there, becoming dry and impossible to wash clean.

When I grew up I would offer anything under that swift sun for one lost day as a child.

*(PHOEBE suddenly reaches and grabs DREW's hand.)*

**PHOEBE:** *We have got to go!*

*(The girls dash to another part of the stage—then stop suddenly. Silence, as they look around.)*

**DREW:** You sure this is it?

**PHOEBE:** This is the address.

**DREW:** It's so clean.

**PHOEBE:** Yes.

**DREW:** I think it's going to be okay. Don't you?

**PHOEBE:** It smells like. . .I don't know. Do you smell that?

*(The 3^{RD} WOMAN appears, as a COUNSELOR.)*

**COUNSELOR:** Hello. You must be Phoebe.

**PHOEBE:** Phoebe Greer.

**COUNSELOR:** We are so glad you are here. Please sit down.

**PHOEBE** and **DREW:** Thank you.

**COUNSELOR:** And who are you?

**DREW:** I'm Drew. I'm her sister.

**COUNSELOR:** Ah, then fine. That is just fine.

**PHOEBE:** Who are you?

**COUNSELOR** *(pause)***:** I'm sorry. I should have said my name. My name is Grace. May I get you something? How about some juice? Would you like that?

**DREW:** Yes, pl—

**PHOEBE:** No, thank you. We're fine.

*(Silence.)*

**COUNSELOR:** It is such a beautiful day. Do you think? That is one beautiful day out th—

**PHOEBE:** Look, I have a problem, I need to talk to some. . .

**COUNSELOR:** . . .yes. *(Pause.)* You know, many women have this problem. Now. How did you hear about us?

**PHOEBE:** I saw the sign. There was a sign up in the bus.

**COUNSELOR:** Oh, good. Yes, we try to reach out. We have signs on all the buses.

**PHOEBE:** That must cost a lot of money.

**COUNSELOR:** Yes, it does.  But we're here so that young woman like you don't make bad decisions.  Which is so important.  So we spend money to get you here.

**PHOEBE:** And so is this going to cost me a lot of money. . . ?

**COUNSELOR:** . . .please. . .

**PHOEBE:** . . .because all I have is. . .

**COUNSELOR:** Please. *(Pause.)* This, right now, is a very important moment in your life.  Do you know that?

**PHOEBE:** Yes, of course I know that.

**COUNSELOR:** We live with decisions a very long time. *(Pause.)* So.

*(The COUNSELOR pulls out a piece of paper and pen and writes, in silence, for several moments.  Then she gives the paper and pen to PHOEBE.)*

**COUNSELOR:** I want you to sign this.

**PHOEBE:** What is it?

**COUNSELOR:** It says, "I promise that I will think very carefully and weigh all of my options before I decide what to do."

**PHOEBE:** Who am I promising?

**COUNSELOR** *(light, attractive laughter)*: Oh, well, you're promising me.  You're promising yourself, of course.  You're promising God. *(Beat.)* And this is a contract, do you see? *(Pause.)* Do you believe in God? *(Pause.)* Listen, I. . .I'd like to just *include* Him in our thinking.  God.  Do you see?

**PHOEBE:** Uh-huh. *(Pause.)* I don't know why I have to sign something like this.

**COUNSELOR:** Because it is important.  This is our agreement, you and I.

*(Silence.  PHOEBE signs the paper.)*

**COUNSELOR:** Very good. I will peruse your materials for a moment. Follow me, please.

*(The COUNSELOR leads PHOEBE and DREW to another part of the stage.)*

**COUNSELOR:** We would like to show you something. Please watch the screen in front of you.

*(The COUNSELOR exits. Silence. Suddenly the lights blackout and PHOEBE and DREW are hit full with a glaring white spotlight.)*

**DREW:** Oh. . . !

**PHOEBE:** . . .my God!

*(Silence.)*

**DREW** *(looking front, as though at the "screen")*: I think that's a hand. . .

**PHOEBE:** . . .no, no. . .

**DREW:** . . .it is, it is, it's somebody's *hand*, look at that. . .

**PHOEBE:** It just looks like jelly, it's bullshit—

**DREW:** That's the blood, I'm gonna barf. . .

**PHOEBE:** No, you're not. I'm the one going through with this, not you, *so you just plug it up.*

*(Silence.)*

**DREW:** That's the head, oh my. . .

**PHOEBE:** That can't be a person. . .

**DREW:** . . .that's the *head*, I can see its *face*. . .

**PHOEBE** *(generally)*: Excuse me!

**DREW:** This isn't *real*.

*Private Passage*

*(PHOEBE stands and faces the blackness.)*

**PHOEBE:** Excuse me! Somebody! All right! You scared the shit out of a *kid*, are you proud of yourselves? Eh? *(Pause.)* Is there anybody—!

*(The lights snap on. The COUNSELOR is there.)*

**COUNSELOR:** Hello. Is it done?

**PHOEBE:** It is for me. I've seen enough. I'd like to talk to somebody now.

**COUNSELOR:** Who would you like to talk to, Phoebe?

**PHOEBE:** I want to talk to whoever I have to talk to—

**COUNSELOR:** You can talk to me—

**PHOEBE:** —to get an abortion. Please make me an appointment with whoever I need to—

**COUNSELOR:** I'm afraid that's not possible.

**PHOEBE:** *Look*: I just want someone to tell me what to do.

**COUNSELOR:** No you don't. You want someone to tell you that what you want to do is right. And I won't. I can't. Because it's wrong.

**PHOEBE:** What the hell is going *on* here?

**COUNSELOR:** We do not perform that particular service here. On these premises.

**PHOEBE:** *What?*

**COUNSELOR:** We do not perform—

**PHOEBE:** What the hell *is* this? You're supposed to be a Woman's Help Service, whatever you call it, that's what it says, it says that on the goddamn *signs* all over the goddamn *bus*, now where is the goddamn *help?*

63

*(Silence.)*

**COUNSELOR:** Now, I see from this that you are eighteen years old.

**PHOEBE:** That's right.

**COUNSELOR:** Now, you have not provided proof of your age.

**PHOEBE:** I don't have any.

**COUNSELOR:** Mm. *(To DREW.)* Who are you?

**DREW:** I'm her sister.

**COUNSELOR:** When was she born?

**DREW:** She was born on June 16th, two-thousand—actually. . .

**COUNSELOR:** What year was she born?

**DREW:** Ummm. . . Nineteen...

**COUNSELOR:** What year?

**PHOEBE:** *She's thinking about it!*

*(Silence.)*

**COUNSELOR** *(to PHOEBE)***:** You are aware that you need the consent of your parents in this state if you are under the age of eighteen.

**PHOEBE:** I *am* eight—

**COUNSELOR:** You are aware that you need the consent of your parents—

**PHOEBE:** Yes, I am aware of that. And what if that is impossible? What if they would *kill* me? Or they'd send me away. Do you understand *that*? *(Beat.)* Do I look *stupid* to you?

**COUNSELOR:** I'm really very sorry.

**PHOEBE:** Look, I have the money. It's cash. Right here.

**COUNSELOR:** I'm really very—

**PHOEBE:** Do you know what we went through to get this? Do you think this was easy?

*(The FATHER and MOTHER appear.)*

**FATHER:** Hell do you need that kind of money for?

**MOTHER:** My goodness, Drew, do you think you really need that many new clothes?

**DREW:** Please. It's a new school. I just want people to—

**FATHER:** All right, all right.

**DREW:** Thank you.

**MOTHER:** . . .you girls.

*(The FATHER and MOTHER disappear.)*

**PHOEBE** *(to the COUNSELOR)*: I cannot go home with this inside me.

**COUNSELOR:** Do you understand? You are under the age of eighteen. So you see, we *cannot* help you even if we *could.*

**PHOEBE:** Oh, my God. . .

*(Silence.)*

**COUNSELOR:** If you feel that you cannot obtain parental consent, you will need to obtain consent from a judge.

**PHOEBE:** From a *what*?

*(The ENSEMBLE MEMBERS begin a recitation. They all wear dark glasses.)*

**ENSEMBLE:** GOIN' BEFORE DA JUDGE, SHE
  GOIN' BEFORE DA JUDGE, SHE
  BETTER WATCH OUT, SHE
  GOIN' BEFORE DA JUDGE

*Private Passage*

**ENSEMBLE** *(cont'd):* GOIN' BEFORE DA JUDGE, SHE
   GOIN' BEFORE DA JUDGE, SHE
   BETTER WATCH OUT, SHE
   GOIN' BEFORE DA JUDGE

**COUNSELOR** *(as the ENSEMBLE recites the second chorus):*
There is a reason why these things have been made more
difficult.

**PHOEBE:** Oh, God, I've never been anywhere near. . .

**COUNSELOR:** I'm sorry.

**PHOEBE:** . . .you're trying to kill me, my God, you're trying to
kill me. . .

**COUNSELOR:** Quite the contrary. We want you to choose.
Most especially, we want you to choose in a way that will not
*torment* you for the rest of your days, and we know that that
happens, now don't we? *How* many times do we see it? Even
—and I know you've seen this on the news—people who
*thought* they'd chosen wisely, discover that they *didn't*, in fact,
and they want to recant. But it's too late. *(Pause.)* I'm really
very sorry. . .

**PHOEBE:** I'll bet. *Thank* you. *(Walking away.)* C'mon, Drew!

*(The ENSEMBLE MEMBERS weave and bob in and around
PHOEBE and DREW, obstructing their path.)*

**3ʳᵈ WOMAN:** ALL YOU GOT TO DO

**1ˢᵀ MAN:** IS WALK DOWN TO ROOM TWO

**2ⁿᵈ WOMAN:** YOUR PRIV'CY'S SAFE WITH US

**2ⁿᵈ MAN:** IN THE HALLOWED HALLS OF JUSTICE

**DREW:** Who are all these people?

**PHOEBE:** Who cares? Would you *c'mon*!

*(POLITICIAN emerges from the ENSEMBLE, begins a soft-shoe.)*

66

*Private Passage*

**POLITICIAN:** I MADE MY POSITION ALL CLEAR
IN THAT OH-SO-FAMOUS YEAR
SEE, NOW WE GOT ROE V. WADE
WOMEN DON'T NEED TO BE, I SAY
WOMEN DON'T NEED, NO NO NO NO
WOMEN DON'T NEED TO BE AFRAID

*(The POLITICIAN falls back into the ENSEMBLE.)*

**3RD WOMAN:** If men could get pregnant the law would provide for chocolate-covered Advil and a four-day work week.

**1ST MAN:** What are you complaining about?! You can *make babies!*

*(2ND WOMAN emerges from the ENSEMBLE.)*

**WOMAN:** Phoebe? Phoebe Greer?

**DREW:** (Oh, shit.)

**PHOEBE:** (Shut up.)

**WOMAN:** Phoebe Greer?

**ENSEMBLE:** OOOOH
UH-OH. . .

**PHOEBE:** Yes, hello.

**WOMAN:** My God, what are you doing clear over on this side of town?

**PHOEBE:** Nothing, I—

**WOMAN:** And little Drew too, my God, how did you get down here? Is your mother here too, where is she?

| PHOEBE: | DREW: |
|---|---|
| I drove down. | On the bus. |

*(PHOEBE looks at DREW, but the WOMAN goes right on.)*

**WOMAN:** Oh, God, I forgot, you've turned sixteen, my God. . .

**PHOEBE:** I have to get Drew down to meet with. . .

**WOMAN:** Who in the world are you seeing *here*?

**PHOEBE:** . . .nobody, I said I'd help her get this thing. . .

**DREW** *(overlapping)*: It's for a socio. . .listic. . .al project at my school.

**WOMAN:** I think that's wonderful. You're *here*, you're not just sitting at a computer. Good for you. Listen, you say hello to your Momma for me. Tell her I'll call her, will you do that? And, Phoebe, I wish I'd had a sister like you to help me with school, maybe I would have done better. *(Laughs.)*

**PHOEBE:** Yes, yes. Maybe.

*(The WOMAN rejoins the ENSEMBLE as it continues to block and distract PHOEBE and DREW.)*

**3ʳᵈ WOMAN:** THA'S A MIGHTY CLOSE CALL

**1ˢᵗ MAN:** AS THEY GOIN' DOWN THE HALL. . .

**DREW:** This is not right, Phoebe. That's a sign. Somebody's trying to tell us this is not *right*, we should—

**PHOEBE:** Shut your mouth or I'll slap it off your face.

**DREW:** I can't lie anymore, Phoebe, I can't do it—

**PHOEBE:** Shut up, you're here.

**MAN:** Help you?

**PHOEBE:** I need. . .I need to go before a judge, I need to get an abortion.

**MAN** *(calling off)*: Don? Donnie! *(Beat.)* George? They don't come here for abortion hearings, do they? *(Beat.)* That's what I thought. *(To PHOEBE.)* You have to go back along the east corridor, it's room 17B, on'y it's not really a room, it's more like an *area*, they're doing construction, some kinda thing.

**POLITICIAN** (*from the* ENSEMBLE, *sings the soft-shoe*)**:**
COURSE, I WILL HAVE TO SAY
WE GOT TO DO THE PEOPLE'S WAY
THOSE RIGHT-TO-LIFERS, THEY VOTE
NOW WHO'M I TO ROCK THAT BOAT?

(*The* 3<sup>RD</sup> WOMAN *emerges from the* ENSEMBLE.)

**3<sup>RD</sup> WOMAN:** Any male legislator who votes on abortion should have a vasectomy first!

**MAN:** Don't mind her—she just needs a good—

**PHOEBE:** Hello? Is there somebody here? Hello?

**WOMAN:** Help you?

**PHOEBE:** I need, I need an abortion, I need—

**WOMAN:** You need to file a petition form, it's form 53G, Modified, you get that on the fourth floor, fill it out and return it to this office. Next!

**3<sup>RD</sup> WOMAN:** NOW WE'RE GETTIN' SOMEWHERE

**2<sup>ND</sup> MAN:** GOT THAT GIRL UP THERE

**2<sup>ND</sup> WOMAN:** TO PICK UP THAT OL' FORM AND

**1<sup>ST</sup> MAN:** START HER TRANSFORMIN'

**DREW:** I'm tired. What time is it?

**PHOEBE:** I don't know. Shut up. (*In the office.*) Hello?

**WOMAN:** Yes, may I help you, please?

**PHOEBE:** Yes, I was told I could get form 53G, Modi—

**WOMAN:** —Underage Abortion Petition Form, correct?

**PHOEBE:** Yes, that's right.

**WOMAN:** Fill it out, both sides, have a seat.

*(PHOEBE and DREW sit cross-legged at the front of the stage, looking at the form.)*

**POLITICIAN** *(singing soft shoe)*: NOW NOW NOW, I NEVER
    SAID THAT
    B'LIEVE YOU'RE TALKIN' THROUGH YOUR HAT
    ROE V. WADE WAS A MISTAKE
    NOW, WHO'RE YOU CALLING A FAKE?

**3RD WOMAN:** It's a sad, tragic choice for many women.

**1ST MAN:** And it takes a Village.

*(The 2ND WOMAN wets her finger and puts it in the air to see "which way the wind blows.")*

**2ND WOMAN:** Well, it takes a pollster.

**2ND MAN** *(sotto voce to 3RD WOMAN)*: Don't mind her—she's just triangulating.

**PHOEBE:** I have to have a guardian *ad litem*. What the hell is that?

**DREW:** I don't know.

*(PHOEBE sighs and returns the form to the WOMAN.)*

**PHOEBE:** Here. I put in everything I could figure out.

**WOMAN:** I'll take it back to 17B and it will be reviewed, your guardian *ad litem* will be assigned to you and that's upstairs, room 520.

**PHOEBE:** Thank you.

**POLITICIAN:** DON'T YOU FOLKS SEE NOW
    THEY MADE IT SOOOO EASY
    DON'T YOU FOLKS AGREE NOW
    MY OPPONENT IS SO BREEZY
    WHEN IT COMES TO SNATCHIN' HUMAN LIFE
    DON'T YOU FOLKS AGREE NOW
      *(spoken)*

**POLITICIAN** *(cont'd)***:** Vote for that evil
    Far Left
    Secular Progressive
    Antifa-Sympathizin'
    Liberal-Fake-News Watchin'
    Bitch
    And you slip in the knife

*(PHOEBE and DREW enter another area, but are stopped by the 2ND MAN.)*

**2ND MAN:** My name is Peter Franklin, everybody calls me Blah-Blah, but I'd appreciate it if you didn't. I am your guardian *ad litem.* The first thing you need to know is what I can do for you, but the second thing is you need to know what I *can't* do for you which, in sum, is a hell of a lot more than the first thing.

**ENSEMBLE:** OOOOH
    UH-OH

**2ND MAN:** I am not an attorney. I strongly advise that you obtain an attorney, though, of course, that is still no guarantee that a judge will provide for an abortion, so. . .

**PHOEBE:** What am I supposed to do? I am in trouble, I cannot have a baby now, what am I going to do?

**2ND MAN:** I am telling you what you should do.

**PHOEBE:** You're telling me I'm going to *lose*, you're telling me—

**2ND MAN:** —I'm telling you how to give yourself the best chance of getting out of this. Of course, if you'd like to go to the *mat*, try harder not to get yourself into this situation in the first place.

*(PHOEBE returns to DREW, terrified.)*

**PHOEBE:** I am in trouble—

**DREW:** Phoebe, come on—

Private Passage

**PHOEBE:** —now will someone *help* me?

**2ᴺᴰ MAN** *(instantly helpful)*: Oh, well, if that's all you want, *meet my assistants!*

*(Raucous music. Two ENSEMBLE MEMBERS join the 2ᴺᴰ MAN. They all put on red noses, becoming clowns. The actors and director are invited to create physical comic bits during the following section.)*

**2ᴺᴰ MAN** *(as CLOWN 1)*: You're just in time — and a nastier remark I never heard.

*(CLOWN 3 blows a slide whistle.)*

**PHOEBE:** I was told that I needed to come before you—

**DREW:** This is nuts.

**PHOEBE:** —that you're reviewing my—

**CLOWN 1** *(puts an arm around PHOEBE)*: We've just been discussing your case.

**CLOWN 2** *(puts an arm around PHOEBE)*: Yeah, that's right.

**PHOEBE:** You have?

**CLOWN 2:** And there's somethin' we don't understand.

**PHOEBE:** You don't understand?

**CLOWN 2:** That's right.

**PHOEBE:** How can that be?

**CLOWN 1:** Don't mind him, he only had twenty years of high school.

**CLOWN 2** *(proudly)*: Abstinence-Only!

*(CLOWN 3 blows the slide whistle again.)*

**PHOEBE:** What's the matter with her?

**CLOWN 2:** She don't speak.

**CLOWN 1:** She does all the silent gags.

**CLOWN 2:** That's right. She's got a gag order.

*(CLOWNS 1 grabs PHOEBE'S papers.)*

**CLOWN 1:** Now, uh, what we don't understand, this here, what this says, you want an abortion.

**PHOEBE:** Yes, I—

**CLOWN 1:** Our question is, "Why abortion?"

**CLOWN 2:** That's right. "Why a potion?"

**PHOEBE:** Why a what?

**CLOWN 2:** That's right. Why a potion? You're a good-lookin' gal, whattaya need a potion for?

**PHOEBE:** I don't need a *potion*, I need—

**CLOWN 1:** Don't mind him, he was strained through a wool blanket. Now, it says here, it says you need to terminate your—

**PHOEBE:** Yes, I need to terminate—

**CLOWN 1:** —and in this terminology—

**CLOWN 2:** Whassat?

**CLOWN 1:** I say, in this terminology—

**CLOWN 2:** Oh, yeah, my cousin, he's in terminology—

**CLOWN 1:** Yeah?

**CLOWN 2:** —takes care of people's skin alla time.

**CLOWN 1** *(to CLOWN 2)*: Tell me, did your mother have any kids that lived?

*(CLOWN 3 blows the slide whistle.)*

**PHOEBE:** Wait, wait, I was told that somebody here could help me—

**CLOWN 2:** My cousin could help you, but your skin looks fine.

**PHOEBE:** —could help me get an abortion.

*(Beat of silence.)*

**CLOWN 1** *(head bowed, bashful)*: Well, gee, you know, gosh, we'd like to help you, but— *(suddenly manic)* —we just don't understand this stuff!

*(CLOWN 3 gleefully tears up PHOEBE's file.)*

**PHOEBE:** Wait! I need that!

**CLOWN 1:** Now that *that's* settled -

**CLOWN 2:** Nothing's settled! Everything's in triplicate around here!

*(CLOWN 3 blows the slide whistle again. Raucous music plays, as DREW and PHOEBE are left alone.)*

**PHOEBE:** Drew, I swear it, I'm breaking apart, I can feel it, Jesus Christ—

**DREW:** Don't curse, Phoebe. Listen, let's just go home—

**PHOEBE:** I cannot go home! What am I supposed to *tell* her? "Gee, Mom, I'm sorry, I can't go stand in front of the clinic with you today because I'm one of the *patients!*"

**JUDGE** *(appearing suddenly)*: Phoebe Greer.

**PHOEBE** *(picks herself up)*: Yes, your honor.

**JUDGE:** Young lady, you come before me, to my chambers, you come before me with this question: Am I mature enough to make a decision such as the one I am trying to make? Can I make such a decision without the advice and counsel of my parents, who bred me, who have given me food and shelter for sixteen years.

**JUDGE** *(cont'd)*: Have loved me as their child for those sixteen years. Tell me about those years.

**PHOEBE:** What do you want to know?

**JUDGE:** How were they for sixteen years?

**PHOEBE:** Yes, well. . .

**JUDGE:** Alcoholism?

**PHOEBE:** No, not. . .

**JUDGE:** Drugs?

**PHOEBE:** . . .no, no. . .

**JUDGE:** Were you ever beaten? Abused?

**PHOEBE** *(pause)*: No.

**JUDGE:** And you cannot go to them for consent?

**PHOEBE:** No, I can't.

**JUDGE:** Miss Greer, this is a difficult time for *anyone*. . .

**PHOEBE:** *I can't do this to them!*

**JUDGE** *(pause)*: What do you expect me to say?

**PHOEBE:** I want to be a musician, I want to be a *doctor*, for god's sake. . .

**JUDGE:** Well and good, but what do you expect I can *give* you—?

**PHOEBE:** . . .I expect somebody to *understand* and—and— take away some of this incredible bullshit—

**JUDGE:** —one moment now—

**PHOEBE:** —so I can get on with my life, I want to *help* people—

**JUDGE:** —Miss Greer—

**PHOEBE:** —not jerk them out of everything they have—

**JUDGE:** —young *lady*—

**PHOEBE:** No! No one is helping me! I am a human being, I am alive, *I'm the one who's here* and I need help with this, and, and, and now I'm just *fucked*, aren't I!

**DREW:** Phoebe—

**PHOEBE:** NO, GODDAMNIT, WILL ANYONE HELP ME, WHAT AM I, INVISIBLE?!

*(Silence.)*

**JUDGE:** It is my opinion, unfortunately, that you are not capable of making this decision, one that calls for rationality, for clear-thinking.

**PHOEBE:** Oh, God. . .

**JUDGE:** . . .I strongly urge you to notify your parents of your problem. They may surprise you. . .

**PHOEBE:** . . .don't do this to me—Jesus Christ. . .

**JUDGE:** . . .you are hereby excused from these chambers. . .

**PHOEBE:** . . .don't do this to me, they'll send me away!

**JUDGE:** . . .you will be shown out now.

*(Silence. DREW and PHOEBE move to another part of the stage.)*

**POLITICIAN:** WARMS MY SAD SWEET HEART
   DON'T YOU SEE
   THE AFFIRMATION OF FAMILY
   OVER HERE, WHY, WHO IS THIS?
   LE'S GIVE THAT LITTLE BABY A KISS!

**DREW:** Phoebe. . .

**PHOEBE:** I don't think I can walk in there.

**PHOEBE** *(cont'd)*: I can't walk into that house.

**DREW:** Come on.

**PHOEBE:** Don't let them talk to me. . .

**DREW:** . . .it's all right. . .

**PHOEBE:** . . .get me to our room, okay? Fast. Just get me to our room, I need to think. . .

*(DREW leads the trembling PHOEBE into "the house.")*

**DREW:** What can I do. . . ?

**PHOEBE** *(instantly serene)*: Sssh. . .

**DREW:** But what can I—?

**PHOEBE:** You can remember. What happened here. Remember it tonight.

*(PHOEBE and DREW look at each other for a moment, then PHOEBE disappears into blackness. Silence. Lights reveal a small shape on the stage floor. DREW slowly approaches the shape. As she perceives what it is, she gasps: it is the form of a small baby—a fetus—covered with what appears to be blood, mounted on poster board.)*

**MOTHER** *(unseen)*: Like it?

**DREW:** What?

**MOTHER** *(appearing)*: Do you like it?

**DREW:** This. . .Mama, this is. . .sick, what is this?

**MOTHER:** It is the truth.

*(The MOTHER picks up the shape: it is a painted doll.)*

**MOTHER:** This should get somebody's attention, eh. . . ?

**DREW:** Mama. . . ?

**MOTHER:** I hear we're going to have a lot of press.

**DREW:** . . .all right. All right. Look, I can't. . .I can't take this in right now, I can't look at that thing, all right? Please.

**MOTHER:** Well, I understand. Gruesome, yes, but the truth of the matter. I thought I'd ask the little Goldberg boy to help. I thought he could stand there and hold it. Maybe we'd get a video and put it on the site.

*(The MOTHER re-enters.)*

**MOTHER:** We're close. We're very close now. The groundwork is laid. Now it's a matter of images. Images. A matter of boring a few small holes into the mind. Through the eyes. Letting the people see with their own two eyes the horror, the —

**DREW:** Is Bobby here yet?

**MOTHER:** Oh yes. He and your father are talking out back. . .

**DREW:** They are? About what. . . ?

**MOTHER:** . . .who knows. Those two. Thick as thieves.

**DREW:** Okay. . .

**MOTHER:** Look at this. Watch this.

*(The MOTHER gets on her hands and knees and begins crawling on the floor.)*

**MOTHER:** You know what I'm doing?

**DREW** *(stunned)*: No, Mama, I don't.

**MOTHER:** Watch this. Stand in front of me. What you see here is a thing called Passive Aggression.

**DREW:** Mama, I know what passive aggression is, please. . .

**MOTHER:** . . .no, no, no, this is the Real Thing, now, come on. (This is wonderful.) Come on, try it.

*(Silence. Then D*REW *stands before the M*OTHER*.)*

**MOTHER:** That's my girl.

*(The M*OTHER *crawls, butts into D*REW*'S leg.)*

**MOTHER:** See that? You're the police. Or you're the Angel of Death (images, right?) one of those hellspawn that run those clinics, they stand there, we are on our knees, crawling toward that awful place to make our rescue. Now. Imagine there is someone like me, likewise crawling on their hands and knees, only because you are stopping *me, they* are getting by you. What do you do?

*(D*REW *steps to the side.)*

**MOTHER:** Exactly. And when you do that, I crawl forward. Now, what do you do?

*(D*REW *blocks her M*OTHER*.)*

**MOTHER:** Precisely. But what is happening over there? *They* are crawling forward. . . .

**DREW:** . . .Mom, can we leave this for the moment, please. . . ?

**MOTHER:** . . .and so, little by little, we make our approach. *Old* school. Do you know what it reminds me of? The peasants who crawl up the mountainside to show their penance. By the time they reach the top, their hands and knees are torn to shreds, they have lost their *blood*. . . .

**DREW:** . . .Mom, please, come on. . .

**MOTHER:** . . .Images. That's the thing. Every scrape and scratch is a wound in the name of Christ and the Little Children—

**DREW:** I'm going to get Bobby.

*(D*REW *moves to another area of the stage, meeting B*OBBY *as he enters.)*

**BOBBY:** Hi—

**DREW:** Hi—when did you get here?

**BOBBY:** 'Bout ten, fifteen minutes ago

**DREW:** You didn't text me?

*(Silence.)*

**BOBBY:** Sorry.

*(Beat. BOBBY wraps his arms around DREW.)*

**BOBBY:** Are you feeling any better? 'Cuz, I have to tell ya, I'm ecstatic.

*(DREW looks at him, says nothing.)*

**BOBBY:** Really? I can't believe—*Jesus*— *(Changes his tone.)* Maybe you're just in shock a little bit?

**DREW:** I don't know.

**BOBBY:** Well, I think we should tell them. You should tell them.

**DREW:** Bobby. . . Jesus. . . Can we just—

*(MOTHER joins them.)*

**MOTHER:** Tell us what?

*(DREW is still focused on BOBBY.)*

**MOTHER:** Drew, what is it?

**DREW:** Nothing, Mom.

**MOTHER:** No. No, I know there's something.

*(MOTHER looks closely at DREW.)*

**MOTHER** *(gently)***:** Oh, my. *(Pause.)* Oh, my. *(Pause.)* I would have thought I'd be able to tell. *(A little laugh.)*

**DREW** *(pause)*: So, Mom, did you know it's hereditary? If your grandmother can't have children, then you can't either. *(Smiles.)* Sorry. *(Pause.)* Okay. I'm pregnant. Bobby and me. We're pregnant.

*(Silence.)*

**MOTHER:** Well. All right.

**DREW:** All right what?

**MOTHER:** Well, it's always a little bit sad and humiliating for all concerned, isn't it, when it happens like this. . .

**BOBBY:** What. . . ?!

**MOTHER:** . . .but you're a good boy, Bobby. . .

*(BOBBY chortles.)*

**DREW:** Mom—yes, of course Bobby is a good *man*, he. . .yes, of *course*, but. . .

**MOTHER** *(pause)*: But what?

**DREW:** This. . .I just want to *talk*. . .this is. . . *(Beat.)* Jesus, why did I—?

**MOTHER** *(overlapping)*: *Don't* come in here and start curs—

**DREW:** —sorry, sorry, sorry. *(Pause.)* I just. . .don't know if this is what I want right now. If it's the right time.

*(Silence.)*

**BOBBY:** Jesus, Drew—? *(Beat.)* I'm going to get your dad.

**DREW** *(to MOTHER)*: Do you see? *(Pause.)* Please say something.

**MOTHER** *(shrugs)*: What? I mean, what do you want, my *blessing?* What should I *say*. . . ?

**DREW:** . . .please. . .

**MOTHER:** . . .*congratulations?*

**DREW:** . . .look, don't *leap* at me, all right?

*(BOBBY and the FATHER enter.)*

**MOTHER** *(to FATHER)*: Well, hello.

**FATHER:** Am I late? Oops.

**MOTHER:** Well, Robert, this little bun in the oven. Eh? In my daughter's oven. . .

**FATHER** *(laughs a little)*: Word does get around, doesn't it.

**DREW:** What?

**FATHER:** (I mean—)

**DREW:** *What?*

**BOBBY:** All right. Now, hold on just a sec—

**DREW:** *Bobby*—!

**BOBBY:** —all right, yes, I had to talk to *some*body, for*give* me—

**DREW:** I'll be god*damned*—

**MOTHER:** I have said, not in this house, I have *said*—

**DREW:** *Yes*, all *right*—

**BOBBY** *(to the MOTHER)*: That's right. Yes. *(Beat.)* It's just, of course, we didn't mean—

**MOTHER:** You didn't mean to. Yes, well, *that's* an effective "life plan," isn't it. And marriage is passé of course, unless you're same-sex, *then* there aren't enough tuxedos to be *had*, so, *now* what—?

**DREW:** Oh, come *on*, what is happening here. . . ?

**MOTHER:** —you'll be *living* together, won't you? How cozy, just the three of you.

**BOBBY:** That's right, we've been looking at these places, actually—

**DREW:** I haven't said *any*thing ab—

**MOTHER:** Well, then what will you do? Raise a child on your own? On what you make, I'm sorry to have to say it. *Very* wise. Or, why don't you drag it to your classroom, have your students baby-sit when they're supposed to be learning from you. What will you—?

**FATHER:** It's probably not a good time to make decisions about this, Mother, it's—

**DREW:** If you all will just be *quiet, all* of you—!

*(Silence.)*

**DREW:** Okay. *(Pause.)* I don't know. . .if I can do this, if I can have this baby.

*(Silence.)*

**MOTHER:** Oh. . . .

**BOBBY:** Drew, come on, you're upsetting her, we haven't decided anything. . .

**MOTHER:** (. . .oh. . .)

**DREW** *(overlapping; to BOBBY)*: No, *we* haven't—

**MOTHER:** What does that mean. *(Pause.)* What does that *mean?*

**DREW:** *I don't know! (Pause.)* Okay? I'm scared. I didn't plan for this, and. . .I don't know if I can do this now. *(Pause.)* Look, I. . . *(Pause.)* Mama. . . ?

**MOTHER:** I believe that, with one exception. . .

**PHOEBE** *(from darkness)***:** I'm in here — hurry!

**MOTHER:** . . .this is the sickest trick you have ever played.

**DREW:** *Trick?!* What is tha—?

**MOTHER:** Robert?

**BOBBY:** Yes, ma'am?

**MOTHER:** Now, this is your little bun in my daughter's oven. . .

**BOBBY:** . . .yes, ma'am. . .

**MOTHER:** . . .now, do you trust her with your little oven bun, because I have to tell you, I'm not sure, after the *last* time she was in charge of a little oven bun—

**DREW:** Mother, don't—

**MOTHER:** —not *hers*, mind you, somebody *else's*—

**DREW:** Mother, don't talk about me like I'm not here, I am *right* here, in front of your *face*, now can you *hear* me?

**MOTHER** *(very calmly)***:** Oh, I hear you, Chastity. I hear you like a *trumpet* blast.

**FATHER:** . . .the hell we bother coming in here. . .

**MOTHER:** All right. . .

**FATHER:** . . .nobody can get along. . .

**MOTHER:** . . .all right, I. . .I thought you wanted a family, *I* wanted a family, I thought—

**DREW:** I do. Oh, Mama, I do. Not now. Someday.

**MOTHER:** Not now. *(Beat.)* Wait. All right. Now, what about adoption? *(As DREW sighs.)* When I *think* of all the people in the world who cry themselves to sleep every night because they have no children, you are *blessed* with this. . .

**DREW:** Nine months, Mama. For nine *months*, I'm supposed to carry this inside me, and then hand it to somebody *else?* After it has eaten the food I've eaten, after it has taken my *blood?* Could *you* think of doing that?

**MOTHER:** I would never *have* to, my darling.

**DREW:** Ah. I see. . .

**FATHER:** Look, are we going to eat tonight?

**DREW:** . . .so for nine months, I nourish this creature—

**MOTHER:** —this *child*, yes you *do*, that is *precisely* what you do—

**DREW:** —and *then* what, Mama? Because it's not just my food then, Mama. It's not just my blood. I give those *gladly*. No. It's a safe and secure home for eighteen years *at least*. It's clothes and school and crying in the night and you don't know why, and it's being better than those sorry excuses for parenthood that I see every day, Mama, and that I *revile*. It's having all the answers to all the questions, because if you don't, Mama, that child, flesh of my flesh and blood of my blood, can end up dead in a school room closet because *the world is fucking insane*—

**MOTHER:** *Don't* you—

**DREW:** —and I am not ready to fight for a child yet.

**MOTHER:** I see. But you can fight your way into his bed, you have strength enough for that.

**DREW:** Mom, I was on the pill—

**MOTHER:** Oh, of course you were, oh, you're so *stupid*—

**BOBBY** *(a nervous laugh)*: Hey, we didn't invent the damn thing, we just trusted it.

**MOTHER:** Well, that is why you take a vow then, isn't it. That is why you *wait*—

**BOBBY** *(smiles)*: Like you did?

*(Silence. The MOTHER looks at the FATHER.)*

**FATHER:** (. . .get those steaks on now, shall we. . . ?)

**MOTHER:** What?

**DREW:** Oh my God. . . .

**MOTHER:** You told him that?

**FATHER:** I—

**MOTHER:** You told. . . . *(Pause.)* You. . .jackal.

**FATHER:** All right, I think we should eat, I think we should sit down. . .

**MOTHER:** I will not sit with you people, are you *joking?*

**DREW:** Mama. . .

**MOTHER** *(a sudden storm)*: I will not spend an eternity in damnation for you, no!  I won't!  Not for *any* of you—!

**FATHER** *(an equally startling outburst)*: We will sit down at our goddamn dinner table, goddamnit!  Like we are supposed to!  We will behave like *human beings*, for God's sake!

**MOTHER** *(almost a howl)*: *NO!* Not for his sake.  Not in this house and not for His Sake.  *GET OUT OF HERE!*

*(Silence.)*

**DREW** *(with compassion)*: Mama. . .

**BOBBY:** It's over, Drew, come on, I'll drive you—

**DREW:** I'm not going anywhere with you.  I'm staying here right now.  You had no *right*, Bobby.

**BOBBY:** I love you, why are you—?

**DREW:** Bobby, go now—

**BOBBY:** Do you want me to wait outsi—?

**DREW:** *I want you both to leave us alone! That is what I want!*

*(Beat of silence. BOBBY and the FATHER exit. There is the loud slamming of a door.)*

**MOTHER:** Well. Just the two of us. What would you like to do now? Do you want to *fight. . .* ?

**DREW:** Of course not, Mama. . .

**MOTHER:** . . .shall we put on a pair of *boxing* gloves. . . ?

*(DREW almost smiles, in spite of herself. She tries to touch her MOTHER.)*

**DREW:** All right, Mama, come sit with me—

**MOTHER** *(wrenching away)*: No. Don't. *(Pause.)* I want you out of here.

**DREW:** *No!* Damnit, you will not dis*miss* me, you are not my *drill* sergeant. We have got to talk—

**MOTHER:** *I'm sorry, there is no time! (Beat.)* Why didn't you talk before? When you were tempted, why didn't you talk to *God?* You know what sin looks like—

**DREW:** *What* sin, Mama? Sharing your love is not a sin. Who said that? *Who said?*

**MOTHER:** *God* says. And *I* say.

**DREW:** Sorry, Mom, I'm not on that old Hotline to Heaven. . .

**MOTHER:** . . .oh, yes, sneer some more, yes. . .

**DREW:** . . .and I wanted something on my tombstone besides Last American Virgin.

**MOTHER:** Get out of my house.

**DREW:** No. I lived here with my sister for fourteen years —

**MOTHER:** What a wonderful collaboration *that* was—

**DREW:** So where were *you*, Mama?! Where *were* you?

**MOTHER:** Get out.

**DREW:** You were all about somebody else's unborn kid! What about your own daughter, THE ONE WHO WAS *HERE?*

**MOTHER:** Stop that!

**DREW:** The day we *buried* her, you said I should come to you—

**MOTHER:** Stop!

**DREW:** —and I didn't have to, Mama, but I did, and I'll be goddamned, you're trying to bury *me* now! Well, you can't, Mama, *I am alive!*

**MOTHER:** Good! Good for *you!*

**DREW:** —SO WHERE *WERE* YOU?

**MOTHER** *(an avalanche)*: I was mourning my life! Is that what you want to know? I was mourning the life I threw away! For *you!* Now, is that enough?!

*(The MOTHER sinks into a chair.)*

**DREW** *(pause)*: Mama. Please. I'm asking, can we find a way to live with this. . . I need you to—

**MOTHER:** What? You need me to what? What could I *possibly* give to you? You are a complete stranger to me.

**DREW:** You're my mother.

*(Silence.)*

**MOTHER:** You would have been the one, you know. (*Pause.*) You think you're the only one with dreams? You think you're the only one who ever felt trapped? (*Pause.*) We already had one daughter and lovely she was. What did we need you for? When *this* is all you've come to.

**DREW** (*tears threatening*): I would *never* say that to a child of mine.

(*The* MOTHER *slaps* DREW, *hard.*)

**MOTHER:** Don't you *dare.* (*Beat.*) Don't try to turn your self-righteousness on me. Don't you try. All your *cleverness.* Such cleverness from the molder of young minds, how *superior* you must feel, eh? So far *above* everything with your intellectual *gymnastics* and where does life *really* begin, and is it a baby? Or is it just some *cells?* You smile and your *fangs* show, and what *you've* decided your responsibilities are, and *your* life is so important. . .

**DREW** (*preparing to go*): Look, finish what you have to say. . .

**MOTHER:** . . .and meanwhile, there is a tiny bloody body in a *garbage* can, well. . .

**DREW:** (*God Almighty. . .*)

**MOTHER:** . . .you just remember, the only blood spilled at your birth was *mine.* The dreams that went into the *furnace* were *mine.* I *had* you, you're *here* now, so you go live your jolly life—

**DREW:** All right, say it all now because this is it—

**MOTHER:** Oh, you'd like me to say the word—?

**DREW:** *Finish* it, Mother—

**MOTHER:** —shall I say what you are—?

**DREW:** *Just finish it!*

**MOTHER** (*calmly*): Murderer.

**PHOEBE** (*sings*): SHE MIGHT HAVE BEEN THE PRESIDENT

**MOTHER:** You are a murderer. A beast.

**PHOEBE** *(sings)*: HE MIGHT HAVE CURED THE PLAGUE

**MOTHER:** You're not even worthy to be called a terrorist. At least a terrorist has a cause. You only have yourself. Your precious Selfishness.

**DREW** *(moans)*: Oh, what must I do. . . ?

**MOTHER:** I don't know. It must be in your mind somewhere. . .

**DREW** *(weeping openly)*: . . .what must I do. . . ?

**MOTHER:** . . .because it's not in the blood I gave you. . .

**PHOEBE** *(sings)*: SHE MIGHT HAVE MADE THIS CRAZY WORLD
A LITTLE BETTER

**DREW:** How could I *come* here. . . ?

**MOTHER:** . . .to make you do what you did. . .

**PHOEBE** *(sings)*: WHO KNOWS?

**DREW:** *She* did it!

**MOTHER:** . . .just what you're going to do now. . .

**PHOEBE** *(sings)*: FOR SOMEONE LIKE ME

**DREW:** There was nobody helping her!

**MOTHER:** . . .with the blood of another innocent baby. . .

**DREW:** That's not how it happened!

**PHOEBE** *(sings)*: BUT NOW

**MOTHER:** Oh, *really.*

**PHOEBE** *(sings)*: BUT NOW

**DREW:** *Nobody was helping us!*

*(PHOEBE can be seen now, and DREW turns to her. The MOTHER does not acknowledge PHOEBE's presence. DREW brings a laptop onstage—then approaches PHOEBE with a knitting needle.)*

**PHOEBE:** Do you have it?

**DREW:** Yes.

**PHOEBE:** What is that?

**DREW:** A needle. One of her knitting needles. I thought it'd be better. I mean, it's better than. . .I don't know.

**PHOEBE:** Give it here.

*(PHOEBE takes the knitting needle.)*

**DREW:** This is so wrong, Phoebe, this is so. . .

*(PHOEBE kneels on the floor, pulls her nightgown up.)*

**PHOEBE:** Shut up. Okay: go.

*(DREW is at the laptop.)*

**DREW:** What am I looking for?

**PHOEBE:** Pictures, dummy, anything. Female anatomy, female genitals, uterus, that stuff.

**DREW:** What about—I don't know—instructions.

**PHOEBE:** No. If I get in trouble I won't be able to make sense. Pictures are better. Just find me pictures.

**DREW:** I'm so scared. *(Beat; then, of the laptop:)* Okay. . .is this right?

**PHOEBE** *(looks)*: Yeah. That's it. *(Beat.)* Oh, man. . .

**DREW:** This is wrong. . .we could try—

**PHOEBE:** Try what? What do you want me to do?

**PHOEBE** *(cont'd)*: Go to *Mexico?* And be back in time for dinner? Forget it. *(Pause, laughs weakly.)* My first surgery, huh? I'm not even in med school yet. Now find some music.

**DREW:** Why?

**PHOEBE:** Just find some.

**DREW:** I don't know why you need—

**PHOEBE:** If I have to scream, idiot. Now find some!

*(Pause. DREW works at the laptop for a moment and music blasts into the space.)*

**PHOEBE:** Turn your back.

**DREW** *(can't hear because of the music)*: WHAT?

**PHOEBE:** TURN AROUND!

*(PHOEBE gestures to DREW to turn around. Drew turns away.)*

**DREW** *(not turning back)*: WHAT ARE YOU DOING?

**PHOEBE:** DON'T TURN AROUND!

**DREW:** WHAT? *(Pause.)* WHAT? *(Pause.)* WHAT?

*(As DREW calls to her sister, PHOEBE raises the needle into the air, then lowers the needle and thrusts it between her legs.)*

**DREW** *(not turning back)*: ARE YOU DONE? *(Pause.)* ARE YOU DONE? *(Pause.)* ARE YOU. . . ? *(Pause.)* PHOEBE?

*(DREW turns. PHOEBE is on the floor, slumped over her knees, the needle between her legs; she is making an odd humping motion, her back thrusting minutely upward, then downward.)*

**MOTHER** *(off)*: DREW? DREW, WHAT IS THAT. . . ? WHAT ARE YOU DOING UP THERE?

*(DREW turns off the music.)*

**DREW:** WHAT?

**MOTHER:** WHAT ARE YOU DOING? WHAT IS THAT MUSIC?

**DREW** *(beat)***:** MAMA! COME UP HERE—!

**PHOEBE:** *Shut up! Shut up! I'll kill you, shut up!*

**DREW:** She could help you—!

**PHOEBE:** What's she gonna do, the laying on of hands? I'll *kill* you—

**MOTHER:** DREW?

**DREW:** NEVER MIND! I'M SORRY! FORGET IT!

**MOTHER:** (You girls. . . )

*(The MOTHER disappears. Silence.)*

**DREW:** Phoebe? *(Pause.)* Phoebe?

**PHOEBE:** Go away.

**DREW:** What are you doing? Are you done? *(Pause.)* Are you done?

**PHOEBE** *(gasping)***:** Go away. Get me a towel.

**DREW:** What do you need a towel for?

**PHOEBE:** Get me a towel.

**DREW:** I don't see what you need a—

**PHOEBE:** Get me a towel, please, I'm bleeding. . .

**DREW:** Oh, God—

**PHOEBE:** . . .I'm bleeding all over the place. . .

**DREW:** Are you all right?

93

**PHOEBE:** . . .oh, fuck, it's everywhere. . .

**DREW:** I'll get Mom.

**PHOEBE:** *No! I do not want her here!* It's all right. I knew there'd be blood. It's all right. People have blood in them, it's all right. Go away.

**DREW:** No. . .

**PHOEBE:** Go downstairs. Talk to them. Make small talk. Keep them out of here. I need some time just to get cleaned up. The bleeding will stop, it's all right.

**DREW:** Are you sure?

**PHOEBE:** I'm sure. It's getting better already. It doesn't really even hurt now. Go away. I'll be fine. *(Silence.)* Go on now.

*(DREW exits.)*

**PHOEBE:** Oh, Christ. . .I. . . . *(Pause.)* Hail Mary, full of grace, the Lord is with thee, blessed art thou among women and blessed is the fruit of — *(Pause.)* Oh, Christ. *(Calling quietly:)* Drew. . . Drew, are you there? Drew? Bring me another tow — oh, God   . . .Oh, God, this stuff. . .Drew? Dr—?

*(Pause, as PHOEBE tries to catch her breath. She gently rolls to her side and curls up, like a fetus. Pause.)*

*(DREW and the MOTHER stand.)*

**DREW:** I think of her every day. She hasn't left me, do you know that, and she never will. Sometimes I can't breathe, I think I see Phoebe. She's. . .trapped, no one helped her then, we can't help her now. *(Pause.)* How we could let her die like that. . .

**MOTHER:** That's not true, that is *not* true. We didn't. If you had come to me—

**DREW** *(involuntary gasp of laughter through tears)*: Yes. Yes, like I did tonight, yes.

*(The MOTHER sits, stunned.)*

**DREW:** I'll call you next week. Maybe you'll pick up the phone, maybe not. Maybe we're just solitary monsters.

*(DREW starts to exit.)*

**MOTHER:** Drew?

*(Silence. DREW impulsively throws her arms around the MOTHER's neck. Her MOTHER tentatively returns the embrace.)*

**DOCTOR** *(a voice from shadow)***:** Well, everything seems fine.

*(DREW walks to another part of the stage. The DOCTOR appears.)*

**DREW:** Good. Thank you. I. . .I guess I'm ready, then?

**DOCTOR:** This way. Please excuse the construction. How are you feeling?

**DREW:** I'm a little. . .what. . . ? I feel like I'm, I don't know, I'm *buzzing* or something.

**DOCTOR:** Yes, where you close your eyes. . .

**DREW:** . . .yes, and there's this *buzzing*, you get that too?

**DOCTOR:** . . .sure, when I get a cold or something. . .

**DREW:** . . .*yes.*

*(DREW sighs, relieved; light laughter. Then the tears come:)*

**DREW:** Oh, Jesus Christ—

**DOCTOR:** Are you all right?

**DREW:** —what am I *doing* here? *(Catches her breath.)* I'm all right. I'm fine, I'm, now what, I'm—

**DOCTOR:** —prepped—

**DREW:** —prepped, yes, so now?

*(DREW begins to tremble, lightly.)*

**DOCTOR:** It's so very uncomplicated. It's safe.

**DREW** *(nods):* Julia said that to me. On the phone. She said it was safe.

**DOCTOR:** . . .Julia. . .

**DREW:** She was very sweet to me on the phone. How long had she worked here?

**DOCTOR:** Not long.

**DREW:** I wish I could have met her.

**DOCTOR:** She thought you had a nice voice.

**DREW:** Really?

**DOCTOR:** Yes. She was quiet. She liked people with strong voices, but she was quiet. When he walked in here, when he shot her, she didn't scream. She didn't make a sound. She just quietly died out there.

**DREW:** God. . . .I hope they catch him. I do.

**DOCTOR:** Well—

**DREW:** That someone could just come *in* here, could just take a *life* like that, could, could, could just *do* that to an innocent pers— *(stops suddenly.)*

**DOCTOR:** Are you all right?

**DREW** *(nods, wipes away tears):* Yes.

**DOCTOR:** Now, we tend to the matter at hand. First, we— *(Sees that DREW is weeping; beat.)* What can I get you?

*(Silence.)*

**DREW:** Is there. . .is there any way to, I don't know, to know if it's a boy or girl?

**DOCTOR:** Why would you want to know that? *(Pause.)* Would that make you feel better? *(Silence.)* Go home.

**DREW:** What?

**DOCTOR:** Go home. You can come back tomorrow if you want, there's time. Only some, so use it wisely. To decide. We'll be here. Barring another unforeseen . . . .well. *(Pause.)*

It's true. You will never be the same.

You must understand that. But you turned a corner quite some time ago and you will never be the same in *any* case. *(Shrugs.)*

And no one else knows what you must live with, eh? In your mind. Day to day. *(Pause.)*

I hope I see you again at some point.
  If not here, then somewhere.
  And I hope when I see you, you are content.
  You may not be able to be happy right now.
  You may not even be able to be sad.
  But you can be content. There is that. There *must* be that.
  You must be content. . . .

**3ᴿᴰ WOMAN:** to touch

**1ˢᵀ WOMAN:** it's a matter of time

**2ᴺᴰ WOMAN:** to bear life

**3ᴿᴰ WOMAN:** and of timing

**2ᴺᴰ MAN:** There is that place

**1ˢᵀ WOMAN:** above your lips

**2ᴺᴰ MAN:** the center

**1ˢᵀ WOMAN:** yes

**3<sup>RD</sup> MAN:** that you wondered of as a child

**2<sup>ND</sup> MAN:** yes

**3<sup>RD</sup> WOMAN:** what's it for?

**1<sup>ST</sup> WOMAN:** what were you told?

**1<sup>ST</sup> MAN:** well, it's where the angels touched you

**3<sup>RD</sup> WOMAN:** yeah?

**2<sup>ND</sup> MAN:** but we don't remember it, of course

**DREW:** just a story

**1<sup>ST</sup> MAN:** *(laughing kindly)* oh, no, no, it's the *truth*

**2<sup>ND</sup> WOMAN:** how you were *told*

**1<sup>ST</sup> MAN:** the spirit's touch

**1<sup>ST</sup> WOMAN:** dusts away all memory

**1<sup>ST</sup> MAN:** prepares you for *life*, do you see?

**3<sup>RD</sup> WOMAN:** and the wonderful thing is

**DREW:** the thing I wonder is

**2<sup>ND</sup> WOMAN:** you can have that memory back when you return to heaven

**1<sup>ST</sup> MAN:** in time

**DREW:** how we wonder at

**1<sup>ST</sup> WOMAN:** a story

**1<sup>ST</sup> MAN:** so you could come to us

**2<sup>ND</sup> WOMAN:** come to me

**3<sup>RD</sup> WOMAN:** take the stories from us

**1ST WOMAN:** before we're gone

**3RD MAN:** before we're old

**DREW:** and after story time?

**3RD MAN:** a matter of time

**1ST WOMAN:** and of timing

*(Silence. DREW sits, head in hands. A CHILD enters, and begins skipping around her.)*

**CHILD:** Cinderella
Dressed in yella
Went upstairs to meet her fella
Made a mistake
Made him wait
How many dresses did she. . .sew?
One, two, three, four —

**DREW:** Would you not do that, please?

*(The CHILD stops.)*

**DREW:** Thanks. *(Pause.)* Do you like the park? *(Pause.)* I used to come here with my big sister when I was, I don't know, about your age. *(Pause.)* What's wrong?

**CHILD:** Nothing. *(Pause.)* You was mean to me.

**DREW:** When?

**CHILD:** Just, I was playing and you was mean to me.

**DREW:** Were. I *were* mean. . .I mean, I *was* mean to you.

**CHILD:** That's what I said. You *was* mean to me.

**DREW** *(laughing lightly)*: All right. I'm sorry.

*(Silence. The CHILD starts skipping and singing again.)*

**DREW:** I'm, I'm not making myself. . .

**DREW** *(cont'd)*: I'd like you to be quiet, or I'd like you to leave. Do you understand that?

*(The CHILD begins to cry.)*

**DREW:** What? What? Why are you crying, I'm being perfectly plain, why are you. . . ?

**CHILD:** Just, I was playing, I didn't hurt you.

**DREW:** I know. I know. I didn't hurt you either, I'm just talking to you, okay?

**CHILD:** Just cause you make a mistake, don't be mean to me.

*(Silence.)*

**DREW:** What?

*(The CHILD starts skipping and singing again.)*

**DREW:** Why did you say that to me? Why did you. . . ?

*(DREW takes the CHILD by the arm.)*

**DREW:** Stop that. Now stop that.

**CHILD:** Ow, ow, ow!

**DREW** *(releases the CHILD)*: Oh, God, I'm sorry. . .

**CHILD:** Squeezed me!

**DREW:** I didn't mean to —

**CHILD:** Mommy's not s'pose'ta squeeze me!

**DREW:** Well, I'm not a Mommy.

**CHILD** *(laughs)*: Fooled you!

**DREW** *(smiling)*: You. . .

**CHILD:** Fooled you!

**DREW:** . . .you. . .you're a little stinker, you are.

**CHILD:** Stinker. *(Loves the new word; traipses happily about the stage, repeating it.)* Stinker stinker stinker I'm a stinker stinker stinker. . .

**DREW:** Hey. . .

**CHILD:** . . .stinkee stinkee stinkee. . .

**DREW:** Hey.

*(The CHILD stops.)*

**DREW:** Where's your Mommy? *(Pause.)* Who's here with you?

**CHILD:** Why you sad?

*(Pause. DREW shrugs.)*

**DREW:** I don't know. I mean. . .I'm not sad, not. . .

*(Silence.)*

**CHILD** *(brightly)***:** Wanna play? Want to?

**DREW:** Play what?

**CHILD:** Castles.

**DREW:** How do you play castles?

**CHILD:** Sit down.

*(DREW and the CHILD sit on the ground. The CHILD mimes building a sand castle.)*

**CHILD:** You take the sand. . .squish it all up like this. . .

**DREW:** Careful. . .

**CHILD:** Uh-huh, very careful. . .

**DREW:** . . .why. . . ?

**CHILD:** . . .cause it'll fall down.

**DREW:** . . .uh-huh.

*(Silence, as they work.)*

**CHILD:** Sand looks like cookie dough.

**DREW:** Yes, it sure does.

*(DREW stops suddenly. Pause.)*

**CHILD:** Needs a door.

**DREW:** Um. . .right there.

**CHILD:** Uh-huh.

*(Silence, as they work.)*

**DREW:** You have nice hair.

**CHILD:** Thanks. Thanks for my hair.

*(Silence. The CHILD continues to build the sand castle as DREW watches her. The CHILD looks up.)*

**CHILD:** Hm?

**DREW:** I didn't say anything. *(Pause.)* You can play here, you know, I—

**CHILD** *(almost casually)*: I know.

**DREW:** I just—

**CHILD:** I don't mind. I don't want to play if you don't. I'm just a kid. I don't have to do anything.

**DREW** *(laughs)*: Yes, that's right.

**CHILD:** There.

**DREW:** Nice.

**CHILD:** Thanks.  I'm leaving now.

**DREW:** Why?

**CHILD:** Because I'm done here.  See?  All done.

**DREW:** Oh.

**CHILD:** You can stay and look at it if you want.

**DREW:** Um. . .you look. . .

**CHILD:** I look like her.  I look like you.  I look like him.  Bye.

**DREW:** What?  Wait. . .I. . .I would want to give you. . .

*(Silence.)*

**CHILD** *(brightly)***:** Lots of things?

**DREW:** Lots of things, yes.

*(Silence.  The CHILD nods, makes a small adjustment to the imaginary sand castle as she muses.)*

**CHILD:** I should have lots of things.

**DREW:** Yes.

**CHILD:** Uh-huh.  Well, you can have the castle.  And you can look at it as long as you want.

**DREW:** I. . .yes, thank you, it's just. . .listen, you can play here—

**CHILD:** You don't want me.

*(Silence.)*

**DREW:** My God. . .

**CHILD:** Okay.  How 'bout, um, I'm goin' over there—

**DREW:** Yes—

**CHILD:** —by that fountain, see?

**DREW:** Uh-huh.

**CHILD:** You can watch me from here.

**DREW:** Okay.

**CHILD:** Bye.

**DREW:** Bye? I—

**CHILD:** Ssh. So, if you want - I'm just right over there.

**DREW:** Right. Good. I—

**CHILD:** Not far away.

**DREW:** Okay. I—

**CHILD:** Ssh. *(Pause.)* See ya.

*(The CHILD begins to hum lightly and moves away. DREW passes her hand over the spot where the imaginary sand castle stood; then she turns to see the CHILD standing some distance away, in shadows. They look at each other. Lights fade slowly to a deep blue, as of night. Then, the lights fade to black.)*

**End of Play**